How to Buy a Home in
SPAIN

More related titles

Buy to Let in Spain
How to invest in Spanish property for pleasure and profit

'Any book that shows how to have a sun-kissed retirement and get someone else to pay for your holidays in Spain…has got to be worth getting hold of.' – Living Spain

Knowing the Law in Spain
A guide to Spanish Law for the British property owner, resident or long-term visitor

Going to Live in Spain
A practical guide to enjoying a new lifestyle in the sun

'Tips on how to get the most out of this vibrant country so that you can enjoy your new life to the full.' – Sunday Telegraph

Gone to Spain
You too can realise your dream of a better lifestyle

'The author writes with honesty and directness. It is difficult not to be enthused by this book.' – Living Spain

How to Buy a Home in

SPAIN

The complete guide to finding your ideal property

H A R R Y   K I N G

howtobooks

Published by How To Books Ltd
3 Newtec Place, Magdalen Road
Oxford, OX4 1RE, United Kingdom
Tel: (01865) 793806 Fax: (01865) 248780
email: info@howtobooks.co.uk
www.howtobooks.co.uk

British Library Cataloguing in Publication Data
A catalogue record for this book is available from
the British Library.

Produced for How To Books by Deer Park Productions, Tavistock
Typeset by *specialist* publishing services ltd, Milton Keynes/Montgomery
Cover design by Baseline Arts Ltd, Oxford
Printed and bound by Bell & Bain Ltd, Glasgow

Note: The material contained in this book is set out in good
faith for general guidance and no liability can be accepted
for loss or expense incurred as a result of relying in particular
circumstances on statements made in the book. The laws and
regulations are complex and liable to change, and readers should
check the current position with the relevant authorities before
making personal arrangements.

Contents

Appendices

Figures and Diagrams

Acknowledgements

I wish to thank two people for helping me prepare this second edition.

Firstly my wife, Joan King, who has lived and worked in Spain for 16 years and has been exposed to the problems of trying to settle people in a country with a different culture. She spent hours translating the Appendices of this book from obtuse Spanish legal wording into common-sense English.

Secondly Les Stock who additionally contributed background photographs.

Preface

Property is not expensive. It is quite different from northern Europe and the choice is great. White houses in distinctive styles are built on estates or scattered on hillsides for use as holiday homes, investment potential, or permanent residence.

Today's Spain is a young, vibrant country. It is barely three decades old since the death of Franco and the birth of the new constitution, and no land is so diverse and enjoys such an excellent climate. It has a strong personality, is full of rich traditions and has a distinctive culture and a proud history.

Tourism has changed the face of Spain for ever. Fishing villages have been replaced with skyscraper hotel blocks. Artificial flamenco, staged bullfights and tacky souvenirs are entertainment for visitors. Yet only a few kilometres inland, villages, towns and cities lie untouched and retain their own distinctive way of life.

Spain has a rapidly expanding economy reaping the benefits of membership of the EU. Major international companies are investing in a country with a stable political government and strong Euro. Yet the old links to agriculture still exist; orange and lemon groves, flowering almond trees, thousands of acres of vines and millions of olive trees still remain.

Property is not expensive. It is quite different from northern Europe and the choice is great. White houses in distinctive styles are built on estates or scattered on hillsides for use as holiday homes, investment potential, or permanent residence.

Buying procedures are very, very different from those in the UK. Forget the traditional approach of putting in an 'offer', arranging a mortgage and asking a solicitor to sort things out. Prospective buyers must carry out research and ask questions themselves, rather than assuming a solicitor will deal with these matters. Learn about the *abogado*, the *notario*, the *gestor*, the contract and the *escritura*. It will make things so much easier. It is necessary to understand the Spanish conveyance system from start to finish. It can trap the unwary in a country where there are many property horror stories.

A new property buyer will to a degree always remain a foreigner. A foreigner may reside in Spain but their heart will be in their home country. They may think like a Spaniard but will never be a Spaniard because the culture of a new country will give rise to different social customs and attitudes. Some foreigners settle down and remain in Spain. Others go back home, their dream of a new life in the sun a failure. It is therefore important to understand the Spanish mentality and to adopt their way of life. Don't dash about; learn to relax, live for today and not tomorrow.

This book is a balance. It is not for the tourist. A legal expert would wish for more detail. An estate agent would not like exposure to their commercial terms. It is, however, a step by step guide to buying a property in Spain, introducing the reader to the country, where and how to buy a property, the maze of documentation, the legal process and how to enjoy life to the full. The book complements but is not a substitute for good legal advice which should always be sought and taken.

It also occupies a unique position in the marketplace. The managing director of a multi-national property company told me that 'The decision to purchase a Spanish property represents a defining moment in the lives of those so motivated and this book would be a most welcome addition to the genre.'

Harry King, Pedreguer, Spain

Map of Spain.

1

Hola y Bienvenido!

The Spanish are open, passionate, warm and fun loving. The Spanish go out late, drink a lot and eat simply. They talk in the streets, sleep in the middle of the afternoon and dance till dawn. They're laid back about life.

A DREAM THAT CAN COME TRUE

Sitting on the porch in the evening, holding a glass of wine, watching the sun setting over the sea, soon to be followed by a visit to the local *tapas* bar for some food and drinks. Hello and welcome to Spain! A holiday home or a retirement home in the sun is a dream, but one that can come true.

Whether your dream is a country house enveloped in vines, a secret retreat for golfing holidays, or a cosy apartment for the family to enjoy and drink too much sangria, all you need is the courage of your own convictions. Whatever the goal, question not the sunny days ahead, merely an ambition to succeed.

Why Spain, why not ...

The first decision is of course – what country? Why not nearby France, the laid back rural lifestyle of Tuscany, the beautiful clear blue waters surrounding a Greek island, the Englishness of Cyprus or Malta, or even the cheap properties of Florida? Why not! People follow all of these alternatives but for many it is a simple choice between Spain and France. In the last few years, Spain has overtaken France in popularity for both holidays and new permanent residents. Why?

Partly of course it's the sun. Cross the Pyrenees and you're in the baking deep south of Europe and the lure of lovely weather is always going to make the sunniest part of Europe attractive. A house in wet and windy Brittany is just too close to England. But it's much more than that. France is a peculiarly old fashioned country. Spain is fresh, new and vibrant. Who wants to spend hours considering the merits of French history or looking in a musty Left Bank bookshop when in Spain you're more likely to spend your time in a noisy bar with a cross-section of society debating the merits of anything that is loud, or where to go to that night for some good food and wine?

Look at Spain's advantages. The Spanish are open, passionate warm and fun loving. The Spanish go out late, drink a lot and eat simply. They talk in the streets, sleep in the middle of the afternoon and dance till dawn. They're laid back about life. Everyone knows by now that Barcelona is cool and elegant with the amazing Ramblas, Madrid is vibrant and cultured with fantastic art galleries, Seville is ravishing with romantic squares and flamenco hanging in the citrus-scented air. Bilbao is no longer just a port but now has the Guggenheim. Valencia has its new science museum.

Yes, Spain has it!

Will a property be a good investment?

For most middle-income people buying a Spanish property is not only affordable but cheap. A well appointed two bedroom apartment can start at half the price of an average UK home. Will the value of the property appreciate? As we start the new millennium the omens are good. Monetary control in Europe is tight. Interest rates are low. Inflation is down.

But care is required, in Spain the price of homes more than doubled between 1984 and 1990 largely because the supply of property could not keep pace with demand. From 1990 to 1997 price increases broadly matched inflation, but since then dramatically increased yet again. They are linked to the economies of other European countries, such as the United Kingdom and Germany, where in times of recession a property abroad may be one of the first things to be sacrificed. Equally a buoyant economy causes excess demand with an 18-month waiting time for new properties.

Spanish house prices may be low, but they are also volatile, appearing to appreciate in four to six year cycles with 2004 showing a slowdown and 2005 a drop. Looking to the long term however, Spanish property prices have the highest rate of inflation in the world. It may be due to a low starting point, but 18% per annum over the last 20 years is good in anyone's money.

Who buys a Spanish home?

A wide range of people buy a holiday home, particularly if it is near an airport, faces the sea or a golf course and the area has plenty of facilities. However, if it is a permanent retirement home then the average profile is of a couple, mid 50s and upwards, whose children have flown the nest. At least one partner will be an extrovert capable of dealing with the upheaval and change, so together they can look forward to their golden years with some enthusiasm.

Eighty per cent of foreigners buying a Spanish home are British. Fifty per cent of properties are bought off-plan, which is by looking at a plan or show house before the property is built. The majority of properties purchased are holiday homes, near the coast.

Most people buy their Spanish home outright. If capital is required, a loan from a bank or a re-mortgage on a main residence are popular choices. Spanish banks offer mortgages at attractive rates. The golden rule is – if you earn in sterling, borrow in sterling and repay in sterling – but the Euro now gives greater flexibility to these traditional guidelines.

It is not only northern Europeans who buy homes on the coast. Spain's growing wealth and fast growing economy have started to be reflected in Spaniards themselves buying holiday homes, although 'Madrid-on-Sea' tends to feature large family sized apartments, in shared complexes, with predominantly noisy Spanish neighbours.

A PICTURE OF SPAIN

Brief history

The Iberian Peninsula, like most Mediterranean countries, has been invaded many times. The Phoenicians, the Greeks, the Carthaginians, the Celts, the Romans and the Visigoths, six different invaders, take us only to the year 711. Then the good guys arrive. They were the Arab and Berber invaders, now popularly known as the Moors, who called Spain 'Al Andalus'.

Dominant in the south of the country, the Moors established a rich heritage around Cordoba where mathematics, science, architecture and decorative arts flourished. Some of the finest architectural masterpieces can be found today in the Andalusia cities of Granada, Jaen, Sevilla and Cordoba. The Alhambra at Granada is universally recognised as being the jewel in a rich crown, one place in the world where Jews, Christians and Arabs lived peacefully together. Their impact extended into the development of farming through the establishment of terraces with irrigation systems and, unseen, the development of a competent political administration system.

Nothing stands still. A re-conquest followed with the foundation of a Spanish state. This led to the voyages of Columbus to the New World. From 1492 Spaniards attempted to extend their rule worldwide by conquering Mexico, Peru and Chile, destroying in the process Indian civilisations, and returning home with great wealth in the form of gold and silver.

This did not last. The next 300 years saw a succession of wars, the loss of its Empire, and increasing instability in government with a consequent slow decline in economic wealth and influence. An increasingly weary nation saw nationalist generals, led by Franco, rise against the government in 1936 and the start of the Spanish Civil War. Supported by Hitler and Mussolini, Spain was an international outcast. In the aftermath of the Civil War a dictatorship was established, with an often brutal rule. A slow, painful reconstruction of the country began. The economy strengthened and started to boom in the 1960s as northern Europe's wealth enabled its peoples to visit sunny of Spain for the first time. The influx of different cultures and international pressures brought social liberalisation long before Franco's death and the arrival of democracy in 1975.

Today's Spain

Modern Spain is a monarchy under King Juan Carlos. It is a tolerant society with many different customs and lifestyles. Since 1985 Spain has been a full member of the EU taking both European and international politics very seriously.

It is a tightly regulated country having five levels of government. The top two levels comprise a congress and senate of elected representatives from the provinces, the islands and the regions. There are 17 autonomous regions, called *Comunidades*, with their own parliaments and governments. This has led to a duplication of bureaucracy, because in addition to its own parliament each *comunidad* also has separate representation from the state. The autonomous regions are further divided into provinces and then into the smaller local *municipio*.

Spain has transformed itself into a tolerant, democratic society but one still trying to shake off the shackles of the era when heavyweight bureaucracy ruled the day. The political scene is stable, pacifist, proud of its role in Europe concentrating on improving Spain's public finances. The country has benefited greatly from the EU programme of special economic aid to poorer countries. Internally it is still troubled by the Basque separatist group called ETA.

Modern Spain as we know it now has been established for 30 years. The economy has boomed. Traditional agriculture has declined. The importance of manufacturing and tourism has increased. A motorway network has opened up the country. Building is taking place everywhere. The pace of change is dramatic, purposeful and peaceful. Its people, so long oppressed, are now vibrant, confident, open, tolerant and justifiably proud of their achievements.

Some facts

Mainland Spain covers an area of half a million square kilometres and has a coastline of 2,100 kilometres. Spain includes both the Canary and Balearic Islands. It is the second largest country in Europe after France. The interior of Spain is a vast plateau called the Meseta bound to the north east by the Pyrenees, in the south west by the Sierra Morena and in the south by the Sierra Nevada. Across the Meseta itself rivers have cut many deep valleys. Much of the coastline is steep and rocky but there is a narrow coastal plain bordering the Mediterranean.

The population of 40 million is less than many European countries. Spain, despite being predominantly a Catholic country, has a low birth rate and a high life expectancy of 75 years for men and 80 for women. Most Spaniards are now urban rather than rural dwellers, living in the major conurbations around Madrid, Barcelona and Valencia. A million British people live in Spain, concentrated along the Mediterranean and Islands.

Castilian Spanish is the language of the country. Catalan, modified French, is spoken in the north east and Valenciano, a difficult to understand regional dialect, in the east. Two hundred million people speak Spanish worldwide, mainly in the former Spanish Empire, making it the third most popular language after English and Chinese. English is well understood in major cities, the Costas and Islands, but is rarely spoken or understood in rural areas. English is gaining in popularity as it is taught as a second language in all schools.

Spain's principal cities are Madrid, situated in the geographical centre of the country; the seat of central government and an important commercial centre, followed by Barcelona, a commercial and industrial city with a large port close to France. There is an intense rivalry between the two cities, both political and sporting. Valencia, the third largest city, faces the Mediterranean and is an important area for car manufacture and for growing oranges. Bilbao on the northern coast is a major modern port and industrial centre. Sevilla in the south west exports agricultural produce such as olive oil, fruit and wine.

The economy of Spain has changed from a tradition of agriculture to that of an industrialised nation. Ten per cent of the workforce is engaged in tourism, 10% in agriculture and 1% in fishing. Encouraged by EU grants, industry is expanding rapidly. Construction of new, colourful buildings is clearly visible alongside main roads while new homes are being built at the rate of half a million per year. Some people have been heard to comment, 'the whole of Spain is a building site'.

PERCEPTIONS

A dream of a Spanish home in the sun is based on a number of perceptions which in turn are based on media information, advertising, personal knowledge and experience.

Holidays

The first perception was probably gained during a holiday on the Costas or on the Islands of Spain. It is a very positive perception with lots of sun, excellent wine and food, new friends, together with a very different culture. The formula is so good that repeat prescriptions are often required and taken.

Life at home

The second perception, probably slightly negative, is of life and work at home. Long dark cold winters, seeing daylight only at weekends. Rain, rain and more rain! When will it stop? Work seems to be getting more and more stressful. Computers, e-mails, faxes and the internet have added to the meetings, telephones and office memos. Company politics seem to have reached new levels. There is a feeling of being in a rut, a change of life style necessary.

Practical thoughts

Of course the desire for change is coupled with a sense of pragmatism. It is not possible to uproot oneself, avoid responsibility and dash off to sunny Spain. What about finances? What about the willpower to succeed? What about parents and children; how will they feel? These issues need to be addressed.

The big issue

The last perception is a complex summary of the previous three. One that says that the purchase of a property in Spain, either as a holiday home or a permanent residence, is a big issue, one that needs many questions answered before coming to a conclusion. Providing motivation is there, a quest for knowledge will continue by reading books, looking at adverts in newspapers, going to property exhibitions, visiting Spain and talking to other people.

The final result will be an overall picture, a true perception of Spain.

PROS AND CONS OF LIVING IN SPAIN

Spain isn't all sun, sea and sand. Living in Spain for long periods is very different from a fortnight's package holiday. The country may be the same, but the exposure to its people, customs, culture and attitudes is radically different. As with all countries there are a few downsides which aren't mentioned in the holiday brochures and are only apparent when you live there. Nothing alarming, you understand, but forewarned is forearmed.

Climate

Hardly surprisingly the overwhelming attraction of Spain is its excellent climate. Summers everywhere are hot, in some places very hot. In winter anywhere south of Valencia is mild but surprisingly around Madrid it can drop below freezing. Some parts of the Costa Blanca have been described by the World Health Organisation as having one of the healthiest climates in the world, a fact not overlooked when promoting the area.

Climate should be a balance. Not too hot, not too cold, a little bit of rain to grow the crops, but not too much to deter people. Some snow in the mountains for recreational purposes but not enough to affect communications. The influence of the Atlantic, the Mediterranean and

Africa produces a varying climate. Northern Spain has its lush green pastures. The Costas offer sun and sand coupled with the clear blue waters of the Mediterranean. The southern rolling hills of Andalusia attract little movement in a blistering summer heat. The Balearic and Canary Islands are always pleasant, the latter very mild in winter. Madrid, the capital, is either freezing or roasting. Cordoba in the south is noted as the 'frying pan' of Europe.

		Jan	Feb	Mar	Apr	May	Jun	Jul	Aug	Sep	Oct	Nov	Dec
Costa Brava	Max	14	14	16	17	20	23	27	26	25	21	16	15
	Min	6	6	8	9	12	16	18	21	17	13	9	7
Costa Dorado	Max	13	14	16	18	21	25	28	28	25	21	16	13
	Min	6	7	9	11	14	18	21	21	19	15	11	8
Costa del Azahar	Max	15	16	18	20	23	26	29	29	27	23	19	16
	Min	6	6	8	10	13	16	19	20	18	15	10	7
Costa Blanca	Max	16	18	20	22	26	29	32	32	30	25	21	17
	Min	7	6	8	10	13	15	19	20	18	15	10	7
Costa Calida	Max	15	16	18	19	23	25	29	29	27	24	20	17
	Min	5	5	8	9	13	17	20	20	18	14	10	7
Costa del Sol	Max	17	17	19	21	23	27	29	30	29	23	20	17
	Min	9	9	11	13	15	19	21	22	20	16	12	9
Costa de la Luz	Max	15	14	18	21	23	27	29	30	29	23	20	17
	Min	8	7	11	12	15	18	20	20	19	15	12	9
Santander	Max	12	12	15	15	17	19	22	22	21	18	15	12
	Min	7	7	8	10	11	14	16	18	15	12	10	8
Galacia	Max	14	15	16	18	20	24	25	26	24	20	16	14
	Min	3	4	5	7	10	12	13	13	12	9	6	5
Sevilla	Max	15	17	21	23	26	32	35	36	32	26	20	16
	Min	6	6	9	11	13	17	21	20	18	14	10	7
Balearic Islands	Max	14	15	17	19	22	26	29	29	27	23	18	15
	Min	6	6	8	10	13	17	19	20	18	14	11	8
Canary Islands East	Max	21	21	22	23	23	24	25	26	26	27	24	22
	Min	16	16	16	17	18	19	21	22	22	21	18	17
Canary Islands West	Max	20	21	22	23	24	26	28	29	28	26	24	21
	Min	14	14	15	16	17	19	20	21	21	19	17	16
Madrid	Max	9	11	15	18	21	27	31	30	25	19	13	9
	Min	1	2	5	12	10	14	17	17	14	10	5	2

Fig. 1. Temperatures (degrees centigrade).

The Mediterranean region has the best balance:

- 320 days of sunshine per year

- 11.5 hours of sunshine per day in summer

- 14 inches of rain per year

- average spring temperature 7 to 27°C

- average summer temperature 17 to 36°C

- average autumn temperature 9 to 30°C

- average winter temperature 1 to 23°C

While northern Europe is being deluged with rain, battered by wind, its roads closed by snow and ice, you can almost guarantee that Alicante and Malaga will be bathed in sunshine. But not all of Spain enjoys a Mediterranean climate. Here are some less attractive statistics:

- San Sebastian – 41 inches of rain per year

- Madrid – average lowest winter temperature minus 5°C

- Extremadura – average highest summer temperature 41°C.

While there may be other reasons for coming to Spain, climate is the big, big number one. It is healthy; makes one feel good and equally important keeps the heating bills low.

Cost of living

Spain is no longer the cheap and cheerful country it once was. The cost of living has increased considerably over the last decade. However, with the exception of large cities, the cost of living is still lower in coastal and rural areas than it is in the United Kingdom, Ireland, Germany and France. It is significantly lower than the cost of living in the

Scandinavian countries and is on a par with Florida.

A dominant factor in such a comparison is the relationship between the pound sterling and the Euro. Ex-pats who were paid in sterling during the first few millennium years received unprecedented exchange rates of 1.7€ to the £. However these are unlikely to be repeated as European economic integration takes place.

Spain's sunny geographical location too affects the cost of living. There is an abundance of locally produced food and wine, not only fresh from the market garden of Europe, but also cheap and plentiful. The beneficial effect of sunshine on day-to-day living costs is truly amazing. Utility bill unit charges for electric and gas may be slightly high, but low demand more than compensates.

Something for everyone

There is more to life in Spain than the sun, sea and sand of the Costas. Only a few miles inland, traditional Spain opens up. The transformation is remarkable as high rise modern buildings, set in clean cities, are quickly left behind to be replaced by small white-walled villages and then, even further inland, by individual white houses scattered over hillsides. One such example is typified on the Costa del Sol where, a few miles from the city of Malaga, the white village of Competa is completely surrounded by thousands of individual white properties nestling on hillsides or sheltering in valleys.

There is a clever tourist poster of Andalusia which emphasises the diversity Spain offers. It starts at the top with blue sky and sun, slightly lower down it has skiers on the snow-capped Sierra Nevada, in the middle drawings of Moorish Granada, Sevilla and Cordoba. Near the bottom it has flamenco and bullfighting, and at the bottom the tourist resorts of Marbella, Malaga and Torremolinos facing a beach and the Mediterranean sea.

Some beer and sandwich resorts, which in the past have received negative publicity, recognise their prime source of income is from tourism. They have now embarked on programmes to attract family groups. Spain, once only home of the package holiday, now has international standard entertainment, theme parks and top class restaurants. And the Costas, home to tourists and house hunters, now have competition from excellent inland offerings.

There really is something for everyone in Spain.

The people

Anyone who has spent even a short time in Spain will know that its people are friendly. If you are polite, smile, and offer locals a greeting in their own language it will go a long way to establishing and maintaining relationships. Polite, welcoming and eager to please is an accurate description of the average Senor and Senora.

Some people have been known to say this friendliness is superficial, asking the question 'Have you ever been invited into a Spanish home?' This is valid and it also would be fair to say in tourist resorts a perceived need to extract the maximum Euros in the minimum time has eroded the natural charm of Spaniards. But it would be wrong to characterise the whole country for the behaviour of a few.

As one might expect, there is a contrast between the older and younger generations. More elderly Spaniards will have endured the repression of the Franco years, may be illiterate and have worked in agriculture. In contrast their offspring will be vibrant, computer literate, with a city based mentality that embraces new cosmopolitan values.

Today, social customs are changing. People are much less formal but familiarity is still a hallmark of Spanish life. Handshaking and kissing on the cheek is the usual form of greeting. Old fashioned courtesy and formality are still the custom in rural areas. Great store is set by personal loyalty and friendship, but it is also very important to take account of a Spaniard's personal sense of honour and pride, which is easily offended. The extended family is the main social unit with family ties strong.

Medical facilities

Medical and dental facilities are among the best in Europe. There are many new hospitals staffed by highly qualified doctors and nurses. A high percentage of the cost of this service is provided from private resources. In addition to the doctor's surgery, the chemist occupies a unique position in the medical hierarchy by providing remedies for simple ailments.

Crime

Spain does have a high petty crime rate. Homes have to be protected by security grilles on doors and windows. Cash, passports and electrical goods are the main targets. The theft of motor scooters is so high that insurance companies do not accept this risk. The police seem unable to reduce these incidents, so homeowners need to ensure protection of their property.

Pickpockets, operating in gangs, are active at all open-air markets, indoor markets and within some supermarkets, particularly when thronged with people during the busy summer season.

It is wrong to point the finger at any nationality, social or occupational group because this is the result of a tolerant society. While murder, bank robbery and crimes of passion are reported in the popular press these are a rarity. As long as sensible precautions are taken, the streets of Spain are safe for both adults and children.

Red tape

Unfortunately Spain is a nation of bureaucrats. Red tape stifles simple daily transactions and frustrates all nationalities including Spaniards themselves. While it is not necessary to obtain permission to wallpaper a room, Spanish officialdom can be all pervasive. When something has to be done, approved or achieved it usually follows a standard pattern – fill in a form and get it approved. It all takes time.

First, there is a queue for the application form. Then a queue to hand it in, only to find the application is not valid unless accompanied by two other documents which can only be obtained from other departments in different parts of town. Once obtained, queue again only to discover that the application will not take effect until stamped by the head of department and he has gone home for the day.

The whole process is made more difficult by the opening hours of the little grilles behind which Spanish bureaucrats confront their public. Not only can the opening hours vary from department to department, but they are always as short as possible. Then there are fiestas, local and national holidays and ...!

It is very difficult to deal with, and most people opt out of the cycle by employing their own personal 'red-tape-cutter' known as a *gestor*.

Culture

Festivals, cultural events and sports events crowd the Spanish calendar. Even small villages have at least one traditional fiesta, lasting a week or more, when parades, bull running and fireworks replace work. Rural and coastal towns celebrate their harvest or fishing catch with a gastronomic feast where local produce can be sampled with liberal quantities of wine. Music, dance and drama festivals are held in the major cities throughout the year. It is called Spanish culture. If however fireworks go off at midnight, a band is playing at four o'clock in the morning and all shops are unexpectedly closed due to a local holiday then patience, among other things, is required.

Manana

The last major downside of Spain is the feature called *manana* – never do something today if it can be put off to tomorrow, or the day after, or perhaps never to be done at all. To live successfully in Spain it is necessary to come to terms with its culture. Coping with *manana* is a necessary skill that just has to be acquired. It is best seen with builders, repairmen, or when a car breaks down or indeed any occurrence requiring a commitment to a time or date. A shrug of the shoulders, an upturned hand, a slight bow of the head, a moment of silence is *manana* in progress.

It is argued that in a large city *manana* does not exist. They work as hard as their European brothers and sisters. Builders work hard, for long hours with full order books. Supermarkets have extended opening hours. The old Spanish proverb 'It is good to do nothing and rest afterwards' (*es bueno descansar y no hacer nada despues*) is no longer applicable. All this is true, but somewhere, under the surface lurks …

SPAIN'S NEW FOREIGN RESIDENTS

While most of Spain's visitors are holidaymakers, some northern Europeans become permanent residents. This early trickle of migrants has become a steady flow, forming one of the main retirement locations for people from northern Europe. For this group of people, climate is important but another important reason is grounded in personal finances, as there are of course considerable house price differentials between northern and southern Europe. Reasons why people may wish to move permanently to Spain, researched by Sheffield University and published in a book entitled *Sunset Lives* are:

- Climate and other aspects of the natural environment such as landscape and clean air.

- The pace of life, feeling healthier, more relaxed, opportunities for golf, sailing and active sports.

- Lower living costs, housing costs, cheaper food, lower heating bills and lower taxes.

- The presence of a British community, many friends, a good social life, the opportunity for relatives to visit and a friendly local population.

- Admiration for Spain, the country's society and culture.

- Childhood or family links, including marriage to a Spaniard.

- Antipathy to the UK, such as high crime or poor social values, a general wish to live abroad or long-term expatriates with no wish to return to the UK.

- English is widely spoken with easy travel to the UK.

A more recent report by an international branch of a UK building society stated that an extra six million Britons will venture abroad to work or live by the year 2020. Their motivation is to reduce stress, as many are working long hours in highly pressurised occupations. These Brits are already looking for and researching destinations that can give them a more relaxed lifestyle and more leisure time. A breakdown of reasons indicates:

- 39% searching for a better quality of life
- 38% searching after new experiences
- 25% searching for a new challenge.

Brits also have a growing appetite for overseas holidays with Spain as their number one destination. This has increased their exposure to new experiences. People are becoming more dissatisfied with their lives and a trend for television programmes such as *A Place in the Sun* and *No Turning Back* emphasises the point. The TV experience is aimed at despondent Brits who want to make a new life, with a new challenge, in another country. They are also preparing the ground for later retirement abroad.

The research forecasts that Britons will constantly be on the lookout to change their lifestyle at the blink of an eye. In the past, people may have moved abroad because of high unemployment levels in the UK – now they may move because of a superficial desire to do something new, for the sake of doing something.

The concerns and biggest worries Brits have about moving and living overseas are:

- 59% said they would probably miss their family
- 47% said the logistics of moving home
- 45% said that healthcare would be a concern
- 37% said language was an issue.

As Europe has easy border controls for entry and travel is becoming cheaper, opportunities will increase for Britons moving abroad, thus allowing more people to fulfil their dream for a new experience. The research also shows substantial differences of opinion between professions, with senior managers citing Spain and France as joint favourites, whereas finance workers, manual staff and middle managers name Spain as their favourite.

2

Deciding Where to Go

The capital of Cantabria is Santander, a ferry port which Brits pass through on their way from England to the Med. They rarely stop. Yet this town has beautiful beaches, international culture and a climate on a par with the south of France.

Before reaching for a passport, a credit card, an air ticket, bikini or shorts; pause. Where do you want to go? When do you want to go, for the seasons magnify or hide some of Spain's more interesting characteristics?

SEASONS

Life in Spain moves outdoors with the arrival of spring. Cafés fill with people. The countryside is at its best as wild flowers bloom before the onset of the summer heat. Water flows to crops, giving a green look to a sometimes barren landscape. This is a good time to look at property. Everything is fresh and clean. Summer crowds are absent.

July and August, even June and September, is Spain's big holiday season. Big cities empty as Spaniards flock to the coast or to mountains to escape the searing heat of the interior. Their numbers are swelled by millions of foreign tourists. Entertainment and eating only take place in the cool of the evening. In the late summer fiestas are everywhere. It is hot, stifling and there are too many people about. Some do go to look at property, but it is an exhausting business.

During autumn, after the heat of summer and before the rainy season arrives, Spain's countryside, roads and properties have a dirty, unwashed, unattractive appearance. A thin film of dust covers everything. Towards the end of this period rain arrives, sometimes heavy torrential rain. The northern tourist resorts practically close down but the harvesting of crops continues, with grape and wine production taking over as the main cultural and agricultural activity.

It is always said that winter is a good time to view property. Another side of Spain is seen as urbanisations (estates) empty; many restaurants close and coastal resorts appear quite desolate. In the high mountains snowfall brings skiers to the slopes, while at lower altitudes olives, oranges and lemons are being gathered. The cold of Madrid contrasts with the warmth of the Canaries' high tourist season. The first rays of spring are eagerly awaited.

MAJOR COASTAL AREAS

The popularity of Spain's coastal areas is undiminished. Its climate and amenities are at their best. Sun, sea and sand! This is the traditional ground for foreign property purchasers, not necessarily just on the coast itself but also a few miles inland.

Costa Blanca

An area distinguished by its fine climate and that prestigious recommendation from the World Health Organisation, it has fine commercial centres at Valencia, Spain's third largest city, Alicante the main city on the Costa Blanca, Cartagena a former naval base and of course Murcia, a lively university city. Tucked away to the south is the almost unknown area called the Costa Calida and to the north the Costa del Azahar. The principal holiday resorts are Benidorm and Torrevieja.

Close to the sea there are several scenic nature reserves – the freshwater lagoons of L'Albufera, the saltpans of Torrevieja and the limestone crag of the Penya d'Ifach. Inland the mountains around Alcoi await discovery, but the green Jalon Valley is now a magnet for over-development.

Having warmer winters than the Costa Brava, cheaper and less fashionable than the Costa del Sol, the Costa Blanca occupies a prime stretch of Mediterranean coastline with Alicante's airport and main line railway station a major communication hub. Long sandy beaches, in places lined with hotels and apartment blocks, are a feature of the area.

There are two parts to the Costa Blanca. The northern Costa Blanca is the prettiest part with rocky coves backed by rugged green mountains around its main towns of Denia, Javea, Calpe and Altea. Benidorm dominates the central Costa Blanca. Europe's largest single resort has an image problem. Build on success they say … and they do, bigger, higher, each hotel more luxurious than the last.

The southern Costa Blanca, below Alicante, one of the fastest-growing areas in Spain for holiday home purchases. Anyone looking for property will invariably come across the town of Torrevieja and Orihuela Costa, the fastest expanding region in Europe where, since the mid 80s, houses have been built at a prodigious rate. In the next five years new homes are to be built at the rate of 6,000 units per year. Selling these homes either for permanent residence, holiday, or to let is a major marketing exercise with companies all over Europe competing with a portfolio of detached, semi-detached, terraced and apartment style properties. What is the attraction? Properties here are cheap, the climate excellent and communications are good. The downside – in summer it is wall to wall with people. The beaches are packed and the restaurants are full. In winter the white urbanisations are mostly uninhabited. Since virtually everything here is new, this is not an area to assimilate Spanish culture.

Costa del Sol and Andalusia

Andalusia is a large area extending across the south of the country incorporating the deserts of Almeria, the wetlands of Donana, the snow-capped peaks of the Sierra Nevada and the beaches of the Costa del Sol. The inland cities of Granada, Cordoba and Seville share a rich Moorish heritage.

There is of course more to Andalusia than just the Costa del Sol. The Costa de la Luz sits on the Atlantic side of the region and the Costa Tropical has sprung up as the coastal area of Granada province.

But it is the Costa del Sol that holds our attention. It may be one the most over-developed strips of coastline in the world, but thanks to 300 days of sunshine per year this area of Spain is home to many. It hosts the jet set sophistication of Marbella, and over 30 golf courses lying just inland. There are many resorts aimed at the mass tourist market, but some of the older developments, just south of Malaga, have a tired, well-worn look, with planners now facing the difficult task of renovation in this now seedy area.

The highlight of the area is unquestionably Marbella, a stylish resort with Puerto Banus its ostentatious marina. Expensive shops, restaurants and glittering nightlife reflect the wealth of its inhabitants and visitors. Close behind is the up and coming Sotogrande, an exclusive resort of luxury villas with a marina and golf course. Estepona is quieter, not so built up and not attached to the long concrete strip that unfortunately is a characteristic of this Costa. Nerja and Almunecar too are gleaming white modern towns, good examples of popular residential areas. Malaga is another fine city with a thriving port; its new shopping centre presenting an interesting blend of the old and the new.

There are other towns but it is best to give them a miss. A home to high-rise holiday hotels, perhaps less brash than it was, and now run down, adequately describes Torremolinos and Fuengirola.

A few miles inland from the coast at Malaga a different Spain opens up. It is the Alpujarras with lots of greenery and many thousands of classical white houses covering the slopes of its rounded hills. Even small towns blend into the contours of the landscape. For a person looking for something different, and wishing to blend into the lifestyle of Andalusia, then this is the place to be. This is the land of the *finca*, a country house surrounded by olive trees, possibly lacking in all mod cons, but well away from other humans. It is rural life... where time is not important.

Some Andalusians chose to live in former fortified hilltop towns now known as *pueblos blancos* (white towns) whitewashed in the Moorish tradition and today working agricultural towns. Ronda is the best known.

The Balearics

Often associated with mass inexpensive tourism, for those turning their back on the bustle of coastal resorts, these islands have their attractions. The countryside and entire old towns lie relatively undisturbed. The Balearics have white villages, wooded hills and caves. Mallorca, a culturally rich island, has mountains to go with its sea and shore. Each of the islands has its own character and climate. Away from the big resorts and foreign-owned enclaves there are towns, untouched stretches of countryside and even shoreline.

These islands have more hotel beds than some countries. They have towns where properties are 75% foreign-owned. But 40 years of tourism has now given rise to a need for change. The locals feel dominance of tourism over local life has become too great. They wish to appeal to a more up-market tourist and move away from the cheap package holiday image. So enter the regional government's tourist tax to get tourists to pay more towards local conservation projects and amenities together with a series of local measures aimed at halting the cycle of uncontrolled building development.

Mallorca is a good choice for living. Access is usually by air, but there are also excellent ferry services from Barcelona, Valencia, or Denia. The west coast, from Andratx to Pollenca and the Gallic influence of Soller, is particularly attractive. Palma, the capital, is a clean, bustling city. So there are two sides to Mallorca. The packaged Mallorca concentrated around the Bay of Palma and a far more refined Mallorca, found along the northwest coast, in and around old towns like Soller, Valdemossa and Deia.

The northernmost and greenest of the islands is Menorca. It has a cool winter climate and can be prey to powerful north winds. Two attractive old towns lie at either end, Mahon and Ciutadella. Tourism came later here than on the other two islands, and around the coast there are still many beautiful untouched coves and beaches.

Further south than the other islands lies Ibiza. The 24-hour club scene brings tourists here each year. It is a beautiful island with distinctive flat roof architecture and a profusion of flowers in spring.

Canary Islands

Poised on the edge of the tropics west of Morocco, the Canaries enjoy plentiful sunshine, pleasantly cooled by the trade winds. The Canaries have extraordinary volcanic landscapes unlike any other part of Spain and contain no fewer than four national parks. There are seven islands. Tenerife, Gran Canaria and Lanzarote are the largest. Housing can be found on all the islands.

The landscape of Tenerife is amazing. The scenery ranges from lava desert to forest, from sand dunes to volcanic mountains. It has beaches, banana fields, and at the centre of the island is the highest mountain in Spain, the snow capped volcanic Mount Teide forming a wilderness of weathered, mineral tinted rocks. A single road passes through the area, passing a hotel, cable car station and a visitor's centre. Artificial grey sand fronts beach resorts on the southwest coast clustered around the resort of Playa de las Americas. Los Cristianios, an old fishing port, lies close by and has developed into a pleasant town along the foothills of a barren landscape. Perhaps a better location is on the north coast near the older resort of Puerto de Ia Cruz. It is wetter, greener and away from the maddening crowds.

The capital of Gran Canaria, yet another fine city, is Las Palmas. Playa del Ingles is a holiday area of high-rise hotel and apartment blocks best avoided. Puerto Rico and Puerto del Morgan on the other hand are attractive, unique, pretty places, quite the opposite to the brash concrete holiday resorts.

Lanzarote is sparsely populated with more goats than people. There is no water. No industry apart from tourism. Solitude, sun worshipping and water sports in a place where time has no meaning.

COSMOPOLITAN CITIES

Life in a Spanish city usually means living in a large apartment with noisy neighbours. There is nothing wrong with this; one gets accustomed to it. Living in a city brings closeness to facilities such as airports, public transport, shopping, restaurants, nightlife, parks and entertainment. Being near to these facilities means property prices are higher.

Alicante

Alicante is a city with a long history and has for centuries been one of Spain's most important ports. It is the regional capital of the Costa Blanca and its main service centre. The city boasts several important monuments, including Santa Barbara castle and the nationally famous, palm tree-lined marble promenade known as the Explanada. The old quarter, known as Santa Cruz, is one of the city's most attractive areas, with its narrow, pedestrianised streets.

Alicante is an important business centre and offers a wide range of hotel accommodation. There are several attractive beaches within the city boundaries. Excellent shopping facilities exist, with a range of department stores, shopping centres and international boutiques. The residential area is popular because of its proximity to the city's amenities. The city also boasts a new shopping area where many of the chain stores are now located.

Along with the rest of the Costa Blanca, Alicante has a mild, pleasant climate for much of the year, although it can be very hot in the summer.

Barcelona

Looking for premier city living? Then this is unquestionably the place. One of the Mediterranean's busiest ports, it is much more than the capital of Catalonia. Culturally, commercially and in sport it not only rivals Madrid, but also rightfully considers itself on a par with the greatest European cities. The success of the Olympic Games confirmed this to the world. It is always open to outside influences because of its location on the coast and proximity to the French border.

Barcelona is a city with impeccable style and vitality, demonstrated by the very best of Catalan, Spanish, and international fashion design complemented by a stunning live arts scene as it regularly plays host to some of the world's best musicians. Las Ramblas is the most famous street in Spain. It is busy round the clock, especially in the evenings and at weekends. News stands, caged birds, flower stalls, tarot readers, musicians and mime artists throng the wide, tree shaded, central walkway.

Barcelona is situated in Catalonia which presents a picture of a proud nation within a nation, with its own language, Catalan, which has all but replaced Castilian Spanish in place names and on road signs throughout the region.

Granada

Granada is a small city in Andalusia, sitting behind the high mountains of the Sierra Nevada. It lies in a fertile plain surrounded by almost permanently snow-covered mountains and is one of Spain's major tourist cities. Granada marks the final stand of Moorish rule in Spain, and also its most glorious manifestation. The Moors were retreating south when Granada was first fortified in the 13th century, and the Alhambra Palace now assures it worldwide fame. It is considered to be the finest example of Moorish architecture in the world. The layout of the grand rooms, gardens and water features can be marvelled at for hours. Built mainly in the 14th century, the Alhambra's patios, pavilions and banqueting hall served the Moorish rulers until their final expulsion from Spain in 1492, the same year that Columbus discovered the Americas.

It is also an important university city and a cosmopolitan place to live. Granada's population is around 230,000, with few foreign residents. It has a typical continental climate, with cold, dry winters and hot summers. The proximity of the snow-covered Sierra Nevada means that night temperatures are often below freezing in winter and cool even at the height of summer.

Malaga

Malaga is Spain's fifth largest city. It is the capital of the Costa del Sol and a major Mediterranean port. It's one of the most cosmopolitan cities in Spain and for centuries has been a popular destination for foreigners, as the names of many of the city's districts and streets testify. During the 19th century, Malaga was a thriving winter resort for wealthy Europeans.

Malaga has been largely untouched by mass tourism and remains a genuine Andalusia city. The city's Moorish history, as with many other Andalusia capitals, can clearly be seen in the Alcazaba fortress and the Gibralfaro castle, now home to a luxury hotel. It has the best amenities and facilities on the Costa del Sol. The city has a vibrant cultural scene, with concerts and other events all year round. It also has excellent shopping facilities. It is typically Spanish, has severe traffic congestion, and is several degrees hotter than the rest of the Costa del Sol in summer, particularly when an offshore wind blows.

Modern Malaga is situated on the west side of the Guadalmedina River around large department stores and a new shopping centre, which encompasses many of the city's amenities, including bus and railway stations. The old town centre, which is full of narrow streets around the cathedral, is being restored.

Madrid

Situated in the centre of the country the capital, Madrid is a city of over three million people and a crossroads for rail, road and air travel befitting a modern capital. Its altitude of 660 metres gives rise to a temperature profile of cold winters and hot summers, making spring and autumn the best times to visit. Those who can escape from Madrid during August make for the cooler north or south to the Mediterranean.

Despite the climate the capital city has developed its own unique personality. It boasts the Parque del Retiro, a world famous area of leafy paths and avenues, a royal palace and grand public squares. Its museums are filled with Spain's historic treasures. The Museo del Prado contains the world's greatest assembly of Spanish painting, particularly the works of Velazquez and Goya. It also houses impressive foreign collections.

Madrid is a city that offers the best in shopping facilities. The latest designer clothes sold in elegant up-market stores. There are food markets throughout the city. The centuries-old Rastro, open every Sunday, is one of the world's greatest flea markets.

There is a good choice of music; classical, jazz and rock competing with Madrid's own comic style opera known as *zarzuela*. Saturday night starts in the cafés, moves to the tapas bars, restaurants or clubs, revelling throughout the night and adding to the city's clamouring traffic noise.

Seville

El Arenal, a district of Seville, was once home to an ammunition factory and artillery headquarters, but now the atmosphere is set by the city's majestic bullring called the Plaza de Toros de la Maestranza. During the bull-fighting season the bars and restaurants are packed, but for the rest of the year many enjoy boat trips on the wide Quadalquivir River. The *barrio* of Santa Cruz is Seville's other district. It was the old Jewish quarter; a warren of white alleyways and flower decked patios, now representing Seville at its most romantic and compact. The maze of narrow streets hides tapas bars, plazas and up-market residences. Ornamental orange trees line the streets, the fruit having a bittersweet taste only suitable for making marmalade. It was however Expo '92 that focused world attention on Seville when over 100 countries were represented in the many pavilions which displayed scientific, technological and cultural exhibits.

Although very hot in summer, Seville has excellent shopping facilities with some European chain stores represented in modern streets. Premiere living is available in this city where all stereotypes of Andalusia meet. By travelling only a few kilometres from the city walls the rural delights of the countryside open up and detached, white-walled properties set on hillsides are clearly to be seen.

Valencia

This attractive, historic city has the advantage of being a few miles inland from the sea. Here it is possible to enjoy beaches as the Spanish enjoy them, as they have never been developed for mass tourism. Valencia is very much a Mediterranean city famous as the birthplace of the rice dish, *paella*. It is also renowned for its oranges. The annual festival Las Fallas draws people from all over world when monster sized effigies, which have taken a year to build, are burnt in a glorious night of pyrotechnics.

With its large car manufacturing plants and modern port, Valencia is an industrialised city.

The largest science museum in Europe opened in 2000 and the Oceanographic two years later. These attractions are a cornerstone of its new development, with the science museum imposing a new landmark on the edge of the city centre and resembling a huge white animal skeleton with glass walls and a spiny structure of pointed arches. The Oceanographic is the largest attraction of its kind in Europe, devoted to all aspects of the sea and marine life.

Valencia is still very Spanish. A modern promenade lined with restaurants runs along the beach for several miles and the area around Las Arenas is very fashionable.

OTHER INTERESTING PLACES

Is there more to Spain than coastal resorts and large cities? Yes! Other places exist, some old and tired, some less popular Costas, or more rural areas wet and green, waiting for development to arrive.

The Costa del Azahar

This is the name given to the coast of Valencia and it means Orange Blossom Coast, which is highly appropriate since orange groves cover the large fertile plain. To the south lies Albufera, a huge area of freshwater wetlands celebrated for its bird life. The rice used in paella and other local dishes is grown here. It is a playground for Spaniards. Spanish families from Valencia or Madrid, rather than foreigners, buy property here. Gandia, Cullera and Peniscola are all historic old towns, popular as Spanish family resorts, busy in summer, but empty the rest of the year.

Costa Brava

In the 1960s the rugged Costa Brava (Wild Coast) became one of Europe's first mass package holiday destinations. Communications are good, the motorway from France enters Eastern Spain continuing through the region on its long way south to Gibraltar. The area is also well served by train and bus services.

The small towns along the coast north of Barcelona are becoming part of a commuter belt to the city. The coastal strip is very narrow because a steep mountain ridge rises up behind it, and most of the towns have a lower, beach half and an upper part at the top of the hill.

It is perhaps better to miss the mass tourist resorts of Loret del Mar, Tossa del Mar, La Platja d'Aro, and Salou. On the coast some smaller towns are well worth a visit together with the inland town of Girona set on the River Onyar.

Costa Calida

The southern end of the Costa Blanca, administered by Murcia, is now called the Costa Calida or Hot Coast. It claims the well known attractions of Mar Menor, a shallow almost land-locked part of the Mediterranean. Nearby is La Manga, a playground for the rich, where pampered sporting activities and expensive homes in exclusive surroundings are the order of the day. Three golf courses and many other world class sports facilities have made La Manga famous by providing winter training facilities for top class football teams.

The main centre is Cartagena, the Mediterranean home of the Spanish Navy, a deep land-locked harbour also used as a stopping place for luxury cruise liners. It is unspoilt by tourism, has many unusual buildings associated with a long naval tradition and interesting Roman remains. Mazarron and its resort of Puerto de Mazarron have fine beaches, a marina and cheap housing for those who wish to soak up the sun and play golf.

It may be bleak, barren and dusty. It certainly is hot, but this is the last strip of Mediterranean coast to be developed ... and it will be.

Costa Dorada

The Catalan coast south of Barcelona is known as the Costa Dorada. It is Barcelona's favourite weekend beach. Sitges is a family resort but has remained trendy, with a thriving artist's colony. Salou is the tourist hub of the area but has nothing to really commend it.

Costa de la Luz

The Coast of Light is situated to the west of Gibraltar facing the Atlantic. Spain's southernmost tip is an unspoilt, windswept stretch of coast characterised by strong pure light – hence its name. Other than Cadiz, which is almost entirely surrounded by water, Jerez the capital of sherry production, and the Donana National Park, an area of wetlands, sand dunes and marshland, the region has little to commend it.

Central Spain

The vast central plateau of Spain is covered in dry, dusty plains and large, rolling fields. Given the attractions of the Costas and the Islands it is not an area where many Northern Europeans settle. Long straight roads, vast fields devoted to wheat, sunflowers and the grape, dominate the region. It is remote, of stunning beauty, suitable for those engaged in agriculture or for those who want to get off the beaten track and go back to nature.

Regions such as Castilla y Leon, Castilla La Mancha, Aragon and Extremadura are remote with towns often stuck in a time warp. Some villages are on the top of hills, some in barren rift valleys, some barely inhabited and some seemingly inhabited only by green tractors. This is not rural Spain. It is certainly not green Spain. It is old Spain.

It is easy to find remote, cheap houses for sale, all requiring considerable work for those who wish to avoid human contact and live life in the crawler lane dreaming of the adventures of Don Quixote for he is caricatured in metal figures everywhere.

Gibraltar

Gibraltar is not in Spain but should be mentioned as it sits to the south of the country. It is part of the United Kingdom but not part of the EU. Economically it stands alone. A strange piece of land, as a strategic entrance to the Mediterranean it seems less important as time goes by. For a small community, isolated from the rest of Spain by artificial political barriers, the future is uncertain. The economy of the Rock depends on a naval dockyard, tourism, tax-tree shopping and financial services.

Green Spain

Increasing numbers of people are discovering the deep green landscapes, the solitude of the mountains and the quiet, sandy beaches of Northern Spain. The Atlantic coast from the Portuguese border to the Pyrenees is dramatically scenic and the mild, wet climate has created lush green meadows and broad-leaved forests. To the west in Asturias and Cantabria, the most obvious attraction is the group of mountains called the Picos de Europa that straddles the two communities. To the east lie the Pyrenees joining Spain to France by a vast fortress of rock and snow. These mountains, set in two national parks, offer excellent rock climbing and good hiking, but in winter, when covered in snow, are extremely dangerous.

The capital of Cantabria is Santander, a ferry port which Brits pass through on their way from England to the Med. They rarely stop. Yet this town has beautiful beaches, international culture and a climate on a par with the south of France.

DEVELOPING A HOT COAST

Is there an area of Spain which within the next ten years will be rapidly developed? Yes is the answer. It is called the Costa Calida, in Murcia and touched on earlier. Pick up an English language property magazine, a weekend newspaper, or even watch television adverts for this heavily promoted area offering new off-plan properties.

To date Murcia is a forgotten area on the Spanish Mediterranean coast. Looking at Murcia's own Costa Calida, with the possible exception of La Manga no well known names can be found. How long will this last? As to the north, the Costa Blanca has the unstoppable development of cheap holiday homes in Torrevieja and further south, the Costa del Sol beckons, now well worn, almost deserving of its poor reputation.

The centrepiece of the area is the natural harbour of Cartagena which was constructed in 223 BC by the Carthaginians who called it Quart Hadas (New City). After conquering the city the Romans renamed it Carthago Nova (New Carthage). Although the city declined in importance in the Middle Ages, its prestige increased in the 18th century when it became a major naval base. It is possible to get an overview of the city from the park which surrounds the ruins of Cartagena's castle, the Castilio de la Concepcion. The port was Hannibal's Iberian stronghold and the landing place for his expeditionary elephants, and he was followed by the Romans and the Moors, whose legacy can be seen in the winding narrow streets. Excavations in the city include a Roman street and the Muralla Bizantina (Byzantine Wall) built between 589 and 590.

The most popular resorts of Murcia's 'Hot Coast' are around the Mar Menor. A few small beaches are dwarfed by cliffs and headlands. The resorts of the southern part of this coast are relatively quiet for Spain. There are several fine beaches at Puerto de Mazarron. The growing resort of Aguilas marks the southern limit of the border with Andalusia.

The elongated high-rise holiday resort of La Manga, built on a long, thin sandy strip, separates the Mediterranean from the Mar Menor, literally 'the smaller sea', but really a large coastal lagoon of 170 sq km of warm seawater. It has a unique marine environment where seahorses flourish, cut off from their natural predators by the formation of the spit. The sheltered Mar Menor can be 5° warmer than the Mediterranean. In the early 20th century its high mineral concentrations first drew tourists for rest cure. They stayed at the older resort of Los Alcazares, which still has wooden jetties protruding from the beach.

A mile or so away lies the La Manga Club founded by an American called Peters, as a Florida-style resort. Residents on its 1,400 well-tended acres, of whom at least 60% are British, have three golf courses, tennis courts, football pitches, swimming pools, restaurants, bars and a five-star hotel at their disposal.

There are plans to raise the region's profile and the Murcia government is going about it in a sound, logical way. New airports and two new projects for the marinas at Aguilas and at Mazarron are planned. Several sea-front golf courses are proposed and 25,000 more hotel beds. Between the coast and the capital Murcia, near the small country town of Fuente Alamo, a grand vision is being realised. On a 600-hectare expanse of gently sloping brown earth, formerly given over to market gardening, two 18-hole golf courses and more than 2,800 homes are planned. It is a tranquil setting, surrounded by largely empty motorways with the Hacienda del Alamo aiming to rival the La Manga Club in popularity.

If you want a hot coast and a property hot spot too, look to the Costa Calida.

3

Making a Start

*An exhibition is a colourful, noisy affair. Orange and yellow
are dominant colours, not only representing the Spanish
flag, but lemon and orange crops too. The babble of noise is
people talking ... Sangria, that mass Spanish anti-
depressant, is usually available.*

READING NEWSPAPERS

Looking for a property in Wigan, Walthamstow or wet and windy ... Then browse in newspapers and gaze in the windows of estate agents. After all, newspapers have large property sections, sometimes greater than the news content itself and similarly a walk down the high street of any town will provide a display of many attractive properties for sale. Browsing may not take place with any specific intent, but it gives a real feel of style, price and location.

Finding a property in Spain follows a similar procedure. Figure 2 shows the many sources of property search information.

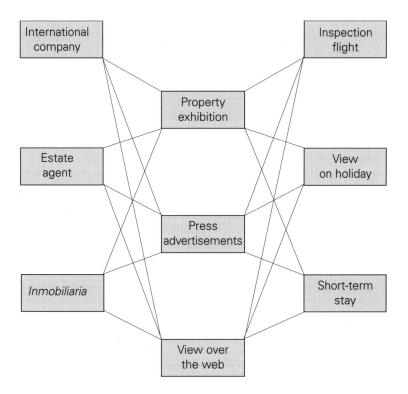

Fig. 2. A viewing choice.

Each week the popular daily press and the Sunday press carry dozens of adverts for Spanish properties. They often have a drawing or photograph emphasising a low cost, high specification property in a sunny location. There are English language newspapers published in Spain too. As you would expect they too have large property sections. Living elsewhere in Europe, it is sometimes difficult to get hold of these newspapers but contacting the publishers should result in one being sent by post. From these you will get a real feel of style, price and location.

GOING TO PROPERTY EXHIBITIONS

Moving from 'passive to active' mode means making a positive commitment. This commitment is the first real step to the fulfilment of a dream. Armchair contemplation is now over. Going to an exhibition is metaphorically 'getting one's feet wet'. Property exhibitions are commonplace; small ones run in hotels throughout the year, large ones in conference or exhibition centres in the spring and summer.

Objectives

Before going to a property exhibition, have some crystal clear objectives. This is not a time to fall for the seductive charms of a salesperson. Nor is it the time to be woolly headed. What is the object of going to a property exhibition? Here are a few suggestions.

- To confirm perceptions about an area of choice.
- To obtain more facts about properties, styles and prices.
- To acquire brochures, particularly those with plans and photographs.
- To ask questions.

- To choose an agent, one who has sincerity, knowledge and a wide selection of properties to sell.

- Lastly, if relaxed about these facts, plan a visit to Spain to look at some properties.

The exhibition

It is a colourful, noisy affair. Orange and yellow are dominant colours, not only representing the Spanish flag, but lemon and orange crops too. The babble of noise is people talking, with much verbal fencing, displays of knowledge or lack of it, or locations being visited or revisited. Salespeople are anxious to 'close'. Visitors are still wary, asking questions, getting facts. Sangria, that mass Spanish anti-depressant, is usually available.

What of the exhibitor? They may be an international property company, or a British estate agent with interests in Spain. What are their objectives? It is not to sell a house since they do not have the necessary detailed, up to the minute information to hand. It is simply to move people to the next step in the selling process, by giving facts and persuading them to go on a ridiculously cheap inspection flight.

VIEWING ALTERNATIVES

It is important to choose the best method of viewing a Spanish property. This cannot be overestimated. There are three options: inspection flights, viewing while on holiday or renting a property for a short period to look around. Let's look at the advantages and disadvantages of all three.

Inspection flights

This is a three-day, escorted, highly focused visit to an area of your choice. Flights are cheap, a hotel is booked and entertainment is laid on. Viewing is from the comfort of a minibus with only a short stroll to each show house. The ambience of the area is highlighted. From the properties shown most people can decide what is best for their own circumstances. It is, however, a pressurised trip, where time and space to think are at a premium. It does not give freedom to appreciate the bigger picture, or the true ambience of town or countryside. It is a snapshot at a point in time.

Inspection flights depart almost every week from local UK airports, normally covering three or four nights over a weekend. These trips, by charter or scheduled flight, are solely for the potential purchasers of a property. Before travelling people are reminded of currency and deposit arrangements to secure a purchase.

Holidays

While giving more potential viewing time than an inspection flight, its use is less focused. When on a family holiday the emphasis is on enjoyment, the area itself and its facilities. Usually, it is only when these are satisfied that specific house hunting can begin.

Short-term rental giving time to look around

Simply the best method! It gives all the necessary time to consider the options. It is no longer a snapshot in time. Property and location can be considered at leisure. But it can take a good few months, leaving this option open only to those retiring or with time available.

INTERNATIONAL COMPANY

Big international property companies have marketing and sales offices in many European countries. Following on from the property exhibition in the UK, the selling continues in Spain with prospective clients moving along a highly organised conveyor belt. Of course an inspection trip is geared to the needs of the individual! Of course the client does not have to buy! Or so they say. Despite this less than obvious sales pressure the package offered by these companies is impressive. It covers inspection flights, property inspection, selling, bank and solicitor selection and most importantly, assistance during the difficult moving-in stage.

These companies tend to dominate the marketplace in which they operate, namely new off-plan property sales. By focusing on this they drive costs down. The huge scale of their operation gives the customer a wide choice. Their influence spreads to property design and development.

ESTATE AGENTS

Few lay claim to the label 'estate agent'. Preference is given to names such as 'International Property Consultant', or perhaps 'Blue Sky Property' or even a more focused 'Torrecasa Property Company'. Whatever the title of the company, it is designed to reflect an image, removed as far as possible from that of an old fashioned estate agency.

And quite right too! No one will buy a new, white, house in sunny Spain, close to the Med, if it is marketed in a dull, boring way. These companies have one or two European offices, but additionally have an office in Spain, or work closely with a Spanish associate. The selling process is again to visit Spain, probably on an inspection flight. Time is more flexible, but the consumer's choice may be slightly more limited.

A word of warning! With such good value for money a Spanish property is a bargain, but it is no bargain if the dream home has been built on someone else's land, or in a protected area, or is being sold by someone who is not the rightful owner. In 1973 the Federation of Overseas Property Developers, Agents and Consultants was formed and is now the UK's primary overseas property organisation. Similar professional organisations exist in other European countries. A trouble-free transaction starts here.

SPANISH BASED AGENTS – *INMOBILIARIA*

It would be unusual for a Spanish estate agent to be at a property exhibition elsewhere in Europe. In tandem with a European colleague perhaps, but not in isolation. They have a curious name – *inmobiliaria*, a word almost suggesting that 'a person does not move'. Yet in Spain these people are commonplace – small local estate agents who know their patch well, concentrating mainly on resale properties. They need not be Spanish – and indeed many are German, Scandinavian or British.

It is a good idea to deal with a registered estate agent. In Spain they belong to the *Agente de Propiedad Inmobiliaria*, have a certificate of registration and an identification number. They can be sued if anything goes wrong. Dealing with such a registered business gives the purchaser more security and confidence.

There are always stories in Spain of people losing their life savings because they have dealt with an unscrupulous estate agent. They may have bought a house only to discover the person selling it did not own it in the first place. One way to avoid this is to deal with a registered agent whose number should be on a sign outside the office, or on a window display, or on the exterior of the building. Grandiose marketing names mean nothing; it's the number that counts.

Additional services offered by these companies are often limited; their main preoccupation is selling property. Some of the most difficult situations facing a newcomer to Spain occur in the first few days of moving into a new home when they are trying to cope with a multitude of issues. An offer of help is welcome. Some agents offer a superb service; their websites are packed with information about local schools, shops, hospitals and generally where to find things.

VIEWING OVER THE WEB

Using the internet to find a property will save time and money. There are now plenty of websites advertising Spanish properties which can be viewed from the comfort of home. Many agents maintain sites which can be found through internet search engines, and more are signing onto property portals for advertising.

Another alternative is to visit a website offering private sales. Direct sales are more common in Spain than in other European countries. Buyers often prefer dealing with owners direct rather than agents because they trust owners more and they have a better knowledge of their own property. The sales price too will not be inflated by the agent's commission.

UNDERSTANDING SPANISH ADVERTISEMENTS

When an advertisement appears in a Spanish newspaper it has a few words of description, accompanied by a photograph. It is 'word art' to describe a home in as few abbreviated words as possible. An additional complexity is the language barrier; difficult enough at the best of times, but in the abbreviated form, even more obtuse.

Example 1 – a standard description

Playa Flamenca Al Andalus 702. Delightful 2 year old duplex. Immaculate condition. Partly furnished. End plot. 3 beds, 2 bathrooms, large lounge, fitted kitchen, balcony, solarium, 82 sq metres. Colourful mature gardens, car parking and communal swimming pool. Price … Tel …

Taken from the property section of an English language edition weekly newspaper this advertisement describes the property adequately. Note the use of square metres to specify size. A solarium is a top floor sun terrace.

Example 2 – a Spanish language description

Chalet, tres dormitories, dos banos, piscina, 80 sq metres, situada Playa Rio, Precio … Tele …

This example is very similar to the previous one, but in Spanish. Translation is not difficult. It means 'A detached house, with 3 bedrooms, 2 bathrooms, swimming pool, 80 sq metres, situated in Playa Rio'. Again the size is quoted which enables the price per square metre to be calculated.

Example 3 – detached, luxury house

Chalet independiente aguas nuevas, parcela 425 m^2. Const 125 m^2, gran salon con chimenea, cocina indep con galeria. 3 dor, 2 banos. Porche, solarium, garaje 50 m^2, estrenar lujo. Precio … Tele …

An altogether more imposing house set in its own grounds. 425 m^2 is again the size, this time of the plot. It has an open fire and many extras.

Estrenar lujo means a newly-built or newly-restored luxury house. Taken from a newspaper, this advert is too abbreviated and does not reflect the true nature of the property.

CASE STUDY

An inspection flight

Mr and Mrs P. were both professional people in their 50s whose children had left home. They decided to buy a holiday home in the sun which could, at a later date, be used as a retirement home. They attended a large international property exhibition at Brighton. Although they considered Cyprus they settled for Spain because it was closer and could be reached by car.

Most of the exhibitors seemed to be talking about new properties on the Costa Blanca or the Costa Calida. One was able to answer their questions knowledgeably, and provided several options and numerous coloured brochures. After a few days' consideration they booked an inspection flight.

They were both acutely aware of the subtle selling pressures. Before leaving they received a phone call, 'just to remind you to have the 10% deposit ready. A cheque will do'. They were met at the airport, put up in a good hotel, wined and dined and efficiently escorted everywhere.

As well as looking at property, their guide stopped frequently at sandy bays, taking them to lunch at marina and golf club restaurants, all with the intention of showing the general ambience of the area to its best advantage. 'We are not here to sell you anything, just to show you around, give the facts,' said the guide.

Later, when discussing offers of discounts and furniture packs, out popped the question 'what is your budget?'

Mr and Mrs P. were fully aware that an inspection trip was in fact a code name for a buying trip. They felt under pressure to buy, but equally in control of the situation, having previously done considerable homework on the area. They were impressed with what they saw, were delighted at some of the properties and paid a 10% non-returnable deposit for a new corner duplex to be completed in 18 months' time.

4

Thinking Ahead

Adults squeeze their posteriors onto seats designed for 12-year-olds. Walls of the room are covered by algebraic equations long since forgotten. Friendly but nervous conversation falls silent as the 7 pm starting time approaches.

LEARNING THE LANGUAGE

It is just about possible to live or holiday in Spain without speaking Spanish. Interpreters or friends can be used as an aid to discussion. The use of body language, pointing, nodding and shrugging can also assist. Enhancement of communication with a few key words such as *si, una, por favor, gracias* (not necessarily in that order) is a step in the right direction. A non-linguist needs one other major phrase '*hable Ingles, por favor?*' (can you speak English, please?).

There can be no substitute for learning the basics of the Spanish language. After all, it is their country we are choosing to visit or live in. We can surely be polite and respectful by learning a few words. Spanish people appreciate those who try and politely smile when we get it wrong.

Spanish business people generally speak English and German in addition to their native tongue. Waiters and shop assistants too can often manage a few English words. Builders, repair men, installation engineers, petrol attendants, postmen, policemen and hospital staff generally only speak Spanish.

How do you learn the language? Home study courses by book and audiotape are heavily advertised. They are an excellent, intensive medium for learning at a time best suited to the individual. Many intensive language schools operate in Spain with prospectuses aimed at a variety of levels in many European languages.

One of the best learning methods by far, before leaving home, is an old fashioned adult evening class at a local school or college. A bit of fun, a common purpose, this together with some effort for 20 to 25 evenings, will get the average person to a decent linguistic standard.

CASE STUDY

Como te llamas?

Picture a typical class. Adults squeeze their posteriors onto seats designed for 12-year-olds. Walls of the room are covered by algebraic equations long since forgotten. Friendly but nervous conversation falls silent as the 7 pm starting time approaches.

The door opens. '*Hola, como te llamas?*' is spoken by a five feet tall, 40-year-old lady with black wiry hair, wearing dark clothes covered with a small floral print. Her skin is olive and her eyes gleam like that of an animal's caught in the headlights of a car. She moves quickly to the centre of the room, turns to the class and again repeats the phrase: '*Hola, como te llamas?*' (What is your name?) The phrase is repeated not once, but many times. It is written on the blackboard. It is repeated many times by the anxious students. Much to everyone's surprise replies are forthcoming:

'*Hola, me llamo*, Heather.'

'*Me llamo*, Peter.'

'Mary.'

The class progresses with repetition being the order of the day. Not a word of English is spoken. In fact the learning process decrees that speaking English is forbidden. The welcome coffee break is extended from ten to 20 minutes with one nervous class member saying, 'I knew the answer until she pointed at me and then my mind went blank.'

The evening proceeds at a fast and furious pace.

Q. *'De donde eres?'* (Where are you from?)

A. *'Soy de Edinburgh, y vivo en London'* (I am from Edinburgh, I live in London).

Q *'Hablas Ingles?'* (Do you speak English?)

A. *'Si, hablo Ingles y un poco de Espanol'* (Yes, I speak English and a little bit of Spanish).

The first evening, returning to school for the first time in 30 to 40 years, is not easy for any adult. The exhausted but enthusiastic students go home to complete, with a great deal of effort, the set homework. *Uno, dos, tres, cuatro, cinco, seis, siete, ocho, nueve, diez, hijo, hija, hermano, hermana, padre, madre, pintora, cocinera, carpintero, medico, estudiante.*

Fortunately future lessons get easier as key words and phrases are assimilated. The 'food and drink' lesson is learnt with ease. *Dos cafés con leche, una tapa de jamon y una tapa de queso, por favor.* (Two coffees with milk, one *tapa* of ham, one *tapa* of cheese, please.)

Learning packages generally follow BBC publications entitled *Viva Espana* or *Suenos.* Adults need all the help they can get to assimilate a new language and this is supplied by a combination of book, audiotape, class work, TV or video.

TAKE YOUR PETS TOO

There is absolutely no reason why a pet cannot enter Spain, or for that matter travel through an intermediate country such as France. The United

Kingdom has recently relaxed quarantine regulations bringing them more in line with other European countries. It may be necessary to travel to and from Spain frequently or unexpectedly, in which case any pet should have the necessary vaccinations, health checks and accompanying paperwork. The website of the Department of Environment *www.defra.gov.uk/animalh/quarantine* is useful.

The Pet Travel Scheme allows cats and dogs resident in the UK to visit certain other countries and return to the UK, without quarantine, provided that certain conditions are met thus eliminating the transmission of disease from country to country. Spain is one of the countries that partake in the scheme. All cats and dogs must:

- Be fitted with a microchip that meets an ISO specification so that it can be read by a standard microchip reader.

- Be vaccinated against rabies with an approved vaccine and have booster vaccinations as recommended. Pets must be at least three months old and be already fitted with a microchip before they can be vaccinated.

- Be blood tested about 30 days after vaccination.

- Wait at least six months after a successful blood test result before being allowed entry or re-entry into the UK.

- Spain also requires an Export Health Certificate to allow a pet to enter the country. It is different from the PETS scheme.

- When in Spain have the pet fitted with a microchip which gives its new address.

Three documents are required to allow a pet to re-enter the UK:

- The PETS certificate certifying that the above conditions have been met before travel.

- An official Certificate of Treatment against a potentially dangerous type of tapeworm and ticks, which must be carried out by a vet between 24 to 48 hours before re-entering the UK.

- A Declaration of Residence to declare that a pet has not been outside any of the qualifying countries in the six months before entering the UK. This will be available from a transport company or from MAFF.

There is another side to keeping a pet in Spain: the heartless attitude of some Spanish people to animals and in particular to dogs, which are often tied up all day, or left to roam the streets, or even simply abandoned. Keeping a large dog is often seen as a necessity for guarding a home, but the ability to bark is not a guarantee of home security. The Spanish are not a nation of animal lovers. There are dog refuge organisations in most coastal towns, invariably run by resident foreigners who often witness many barbaric acts committed on these defenceless animals.

Spain has the normal catteries and kennels. It has many fully qualified veterinary surgeons. Some urbanisations, towns and cities have codes of behaviour for dogs which result in them being banned from beaches and other public places.

LETTING THE HOUSE BACK HOME

Some people, having purchased a Spanish home with the intention of living there permanently, are reluctant to immediately sell their old home. No matter the care or planning that has gone into the selection of a new home in the sun, it may not work out. Retaining a base back home reduces this risk, offering a bolt hole in the event of any change in circumstance. There are two major reasons for letting out a property: income and security as an empty property is potentially at risk during dark winter months.

It makes sense to put the letting of a property in the hands of experts. The Association of Residential Agents, formed in 1981, regulates letting agents and seeks to promote the provision of high standards of service to both landlords and tenants. Membership is restricted to those letting agents who can demonstrate good financial practices and whose staff has a good working knowledge of all the legal issues involved.

There are three main types of letting service; letting only, letting and rent collection, letting and full management. Cost and risk should determine the service selected. The greater the service, the greater the cost and the less risk of unsavoury tenants or damage to the property and its fittings. A letting company will charge around 15% of the rental income for a full service, together with additional charges for introducing tenants and drawing up agreements. Taxation and letting charges can therefore reduce gross letting income by 30 to 40%.

If the owner is classed as an overseas resident for tax purposes, the letting company is responsible for deducting income tax at base rate on the rental income, unless the Inland Revenue provides a tax exemption certificate.

MOVING YOUR FURNITURE

Spanish furniture is attractive, distinctive and ornate, but is not to everyone's taste. Moving comfortable furniture from home, bits and pieces that one has grown accustomed to, is often preferred.

European removal companies are sound professional organisations normally belonging to the International Federation of Furniture Removers. They have well-established procedures both operationally and administratively. The packing and paperwork are best left to them. While it is obvious that more than one competitive quote is necessary, the cheapest company should be one which offers a shared service with depots close to both the old home and a new Spanish home. The cost of moving an average home, including insurance, calculated according to the number of cubic metres required is around 3,500 to 5,000 Euros. Cost reduction is best achieved by flexibility in pick-up and delivery dates. Transit time is approximately two weeks.

It is wise to leave TV sets at home as the Spanish sound system and the receiving frequency differ from other European countries. Washing machines work successfully but the plumbing of a Spanish home does not allow for a hot water fill. Computers, vacuum cleaners and other domestic items all operate successfully on Spanish voltages.

ORGANISING YOUR TRAVEL

There are daily scheduled flights to Spain by recognised national carriers. Standard fares are charged. However, the cheapest and most frequently used method of air travel is a charter flight or low cost carrier at around 70 Euros one way. Tickets are best obtained from a flight only shop, direct from a low cost carrier, or through the many internet sites devoted to flight bookings. Alicante, Malaga, Majorca and Tenerife are the most frequently used Spanish airports.

One excellent guide to getting there is contained in the monthly magazine *Spain*. It contains details of carriers, airports they operate from and to, frequency and contact details. Ferry services too are highlighted.

It makes sense to pre-book car hire at the same time as booking air tickets. It avoids delay on arrival, as the car will be ready. All the international car hire companies operate in Spain together with many Spanish national and regional operators. It is a fiercely competitive market.

ANNUAL RUNNING COSTS OF A SPANISH HOME

Running costs will vary according to the size of a property. As a guide let's take a retired couple, living all year round in a three bedroom house on an urbanisation, with limited heating and no swimming pool.

Telephone/internet	800 Euros
Electricity	700 Euros
Gas	200 Euros
Water	200 Euros
House/property insurance	150 Euros
Local taxes (*IBI*)	200 Euros
National tax (property only)	800 Euros
Community charge	250 Euros
Total	**3,300 Euros per year**

This relatively low domestic bill is a reflection of living in a warm climate with low energy needs. But there are other items of expenditure, not strictly related to maintaining a home, such as medical insurance, and motoring costs which also need to be taken into account.

> Medical insurance 800 Euros per person per year, dependent on age
> Motoring costs 5,000 Euros per year to cover fuel, insurance and depreciation, all variable

OPENING A SPANISH BANK ACCOUNT

One of the very first things necessary in the house buying process is to open a bank account. Spanish banks have improved dramatically over the last few years, becoming very European in their outlook. They are very modern, open between 8.30 and 14.30 Monday to Friday and between October to April on a Saturday morning. The staff are friendly and multilingual.

Opening a bank account is perfectly straightforward but may take a few days. A new cheque book has the words printed at the top, *Cuenta en Euros de no Residente*. This indicates the Spanish banking system distinguishes residents from non-residents for tax purposes.

Inserting English or German credit cards into a Spanish ATM results in the instructions coming up in an appropriate language – very clever. UK credit cards can also be used in Spain for normal transactions but photographic proof of identity is sometimes necessary when presenting a card. This is normally a passport, but it is inconvenient to carry a passport everywhere, so a better solution is the new style UK photo card driving license. As a result of the requirement to produce photo-identity, credit card fraud is low in Spain.

5

What Property, Which Location?

Overlooking orange and lemon groves! Close to a pine filled ravine! At the edge of purple hills! Next to a marina! More simply it can be exotic gardens or a house that has obviously been well loved and cared for. Location is that little bit extra which makes a property highly desirable – and probably that little bit more expensive.

PROPERTY DESCRIPTIONS

Descriptions of new properties in Spain, on an urbanisation, or those chosen from a builder's catalogue, can have names such as Fiesta, Coral, Carmen, Fortuna, Bellavista, Alba, Neptuno, Perla and Rosa, to name but a few. This identity is interesting but irrelevant. Surprisingly, these original names are retained for many years.

An agent's literature for off-plan properties should have a photograph, a plan drawing, a location indicator and a brief description. The size of the plot, the constructed area, room sizes and the size of any solarium or terrace are all quoted in square metres. The price is stated, but usually on a separate sheet, as it is subject to change. A resale property will also have photographs, details of the property including its size, in square metres.

In the UK we have grown accustomed to property descriptions such as apartment, terrace and town house, semi-detached, detached and bungalow. In Spain descriptive terms are usually apartment, linked (another name for terraced), town house, duplex, corner duplex, corner bungalow, semi-detached, and detached which includes a bungalow. The word 'villa' is often simply used to describe a 'detached house' and the words 'chalet style' indicate a single storey property having a porch with a roof overhang.

In building terminology 'duplex' means a house with an internal staircase built on two levels and a corner duplex is a grouping of four houses, each on two floors, joined together in a rectangle. Similarly a corner bungalow is a grouping of four single storey houses joined in a rectangle. Occasionally a block of homes are built together comprising six, eight or even 12 units, in all different sizes and configurations. Although they are known by their individual names, they are apartments, sometimes duplex apartments.

URBANISATIONS AND COMMUNITIES

Urbanisations

Spain is a land of urbanisations, which is a continental name for housing estates. They may line the beach, be in the country, attached to towns, villages or resorts, they may be on flat land, on hills or around sporting facilities such as golf courses. They can be high-density estates of identical white properties, or small individual developments of big detached houses spread over a hillside. More likely, they will be various combinations in between.

A property on an urbanisation is easy to buy and maintain having all the necessary facilities, ready-made social contacts and greater security than owning a detached home in a more remote location. Disadvantages can be the inflexible and restrictive community rules, difficult neighbours, a lack of privacy and a lack of control over the future of a development.

Life on an urbanisation can however be pleasant whatever the type of house. Sitting by the swimming pool meeting new continental friends, passing the time of day with a glass of wine in hand is an agreeable way of life. Little Spanish is spoken. Sharing experiences bonds the community together. Informal groupings take place. Golfing partners come together. Coffee mornings just happen. Family problems are shared. The siesta is forgotten as people assemble in the local bar to escape the searing heat of the afternoon sun. Life is easy. However it is very important for mind and body to stay active or a slow soporific mental decline will occur.

Some urbanisations are closed communities where people meet up at night and get to know each other's business. Others are less intrusive. Some are entirely of one nationality while others are more mixed. In some most of the residents are elderly. Some urbanisations are a group of holiday homes scarcely having any permanent residents, and becoming virtual ghost towns in winter.

Behaviour standards need to be set. An urbanisation is a community by itself where the level is set by the standard of the lowest.

Community property

What is a community property? The answer is one that involves homes with a shared element. An example would be apartments, or a grouping of individual homes. Urbanisations have a shared element in the swimming pool or gardens. Apartments have a shared element in the lift. Detached properties may have a common access road.

The cost of maintaining these elements is shared between the owners. The most expensive shared element is normally the swimming pool, followed by gardens and satellite TV. Spanish town hall services are limited, with elements such as street cleaning being part of the community costs.

A *comunidad de propietarios* can be run by an independent company on behalf of the owners or, in a well organised community, by the owners themselves. Germans have a talent for this; the Spanish an eye for detail; the Scandinavians are laid back; the British and Irish seem happy to leave it to others. Annual meetings are often long and argumentative as many nationalities, resident and non-resident, seek to have a voice. There is a Spanish law that surrounds communities. It has a strange title – the Law of Horizontal Property.

LIVING BY THE SEA, INLAND OR IN THE COUNTRY

By the sea

This is a pleasant experience with cool afternoon breezes taking the sting out of the searing summer heat. But nearly all Mediterranean towns are tourist areas. In July and August, with temperatures always in excess of 30°, people pour in on package holidays. Spaniards too have their summer holiday then, as they rush to the coast in their thousands from the torrid heat of the big cities. For two frustrating months beaches are packed, roads jammed, car parks full and tempers frayed.

Mention should be made of Spain's 'Law of the Coasts', which empowers local authorities to restrict the number, height and density of buildings within 100 metres of the high water mark and to establish a zone of influence as far inward as one kilometre. Despite this, properties continue to be built close to beaches. They do, however, command a hefty premium, the price only kept low by high density designs.

In the country

Living in the country has many attractions. It is living in the real Spain. Large plots of land give peace with privacy assured. Neighbours, although far apart, are normally friendly. Some of these properties have no electricity, no water, no sewage disposal, no gas and no telephone. All can be compensated for by other means. Electricity can be supplied by a generator, or by solar panels. Water can be delivered by tanker or from a well. A septic tank takes care of sewage. Bottles supply gas. Communications can be by mobile or radio telephone and by internet.

Many country properties are large and set in beautiful locations – often at the end of a pot-holed dirt track. When it rains the dirt track turns into mud and a 4x4 is necessary just to reach the house. Is it possible to cope with absolute peace and tranquility after city life … and the frustrations of driving all the way to the nearest supermarket to find on returning that an important item has been forgotten?

Inland

Living inland is a balance. Access to both coast and mountains. A view of the Med and a smell of the country. The best of both worlds and many people are starting to realise it. Inland properties normally cost less than coastal properties … but things are changing with inland properties now increasing in value at a faster rate as people discover the secret of Spanish living.

SELECTING THE RIGHT LOCATION

Although it is possible to choose a region of Spain that is attractive, deciding on a particular town, village, development or hillside to purchase a property for personal use involves a whole series of individual choices. The key to a successful property purchase is definitely its location. It is by far the most important decision to be made. Location will also be a major factor in the price paid for a property; a villa close to a golf course will cost far more than an apartment inland.

Age comes into it too! A spectacular mountain track that provides the only access to a restored farmhouse may seem an attraction when in full health, but is not so good when driving up and down it 20 years later. Access to public transport and medical services will become more important too, and the closeness of other ex-pats, who were avoided in earlier years, may become more comforting.

Some basic questions have to be asked.

- How far away from the summer crowd do you really want to be? Tourist towns can become massively crowded. If you do not want this, look further inland. Most people find a 30-minute journey to the beach resorts or larger towns quite convenient.

- You may wish your property to be close to local shops, bars and restaurants, public transport, a good beach, golf and other sports facilities, arts and entertainment.

- Is the choice city, rural or perhaps Green Spain?

- Do you seek a remote location? This can be a problem. Where are the nearest bus, coach and train services? How good are the roads? How easy is it to connect to the motorway network?

- How many local facilities stay open in the winter? This is particularly important if you are considering moving to a tourist area where there is a big difference between high and low season.

- Is being close to a beach and holiday entertainment important? If that's what you want then look no further than the Mediterranean Costas or the two groups of islands, the Balearics and the Canaries.

- How much sun do you need? For reliable mainland sunshine stay south of Valencia or in the Canaries.

- Is having neighbours an important issue? So many Spanish properties are in an apartment or on a high-density urbanisation. Some holiday home urbanisations, deserted in winter, have no neighbours for long periods.

- How close do you really want to be to compatriots? There are British communities that are isolated from every aspect of Spanish life. On the other hand there are towns and villages just inland with smaller, more mixed communities.

- Do you have any special interests or hobbies? Is this a good location for you? What social life exists and will it suit you? Most of all – will you be happy here?

PROS AND CONS OF EACH HOUSE TYPE

Apartment

An apartment offers easy living in secure surroundings. Apartments are always built to a high standard with outside balconies included. Some economy flats exist where low-cost living is a priority in large cities or for holiday rental. Apartments are cheap, easy to resell, but often attract high community charges. Living in an apartment will probably mean Spanish neighbours. Nice people they may well be, but they tend to be noisy and have a different 'body clock' to other nationalities. Normal behaviour is to rise late, have lunch at 2 pm, an evening meal at 9 pm and go to bed at midnight or after. Family discussion can be loud, very loud, Spanish voices having a unique ability to penetrate all bricks and mortar.

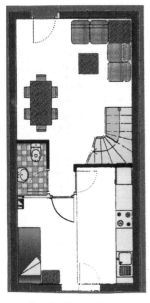

Fig. 3. Plan of a terraced property.

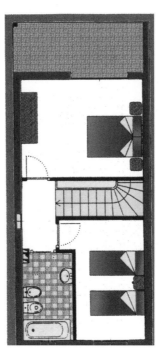

Linked, terraced and town houses

Some of the most attractive new designs are for linked and terraced houses (see Figure 3). These houses are on two levels with a third floor roof utilised as a solarium. They too are cheap and easy to resell but lack privacy. Town houses are available new, but can be older reformed traditional properties in the narrow streets of a Spanish town where car parking is a problem.

Corner properties

Corner housing is mostly found in a duplex design but can also apply to single level homes (see Figure 4). It is a cheap form of building having few external walls. Services,

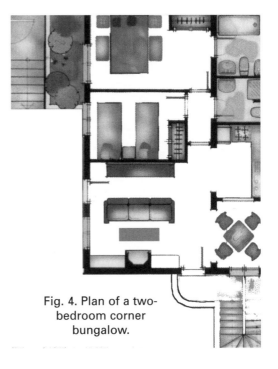

Fig. 4. Plan of a two-bedroom corner bungalow.

although individual to each home, do have some common elements. Corner duplexes are noisy, but their main function is holiday homes, with neighbours rarely meeting. (See Figure 5 for a duplex corner – details of the property can be found in the appendices.)

Detached

These properties offer privacy at the expense of security. They can be expensive. Built to an individual design they are sometimes perched precariously on hillsides, so much so that insurance companies charge a premium for cover. Windswept plots make dust a perpetual irritant. However even with some disadvantages a detached property is desirable, particularly one that overlooks the sea or the mountains or even a lush green golf course.

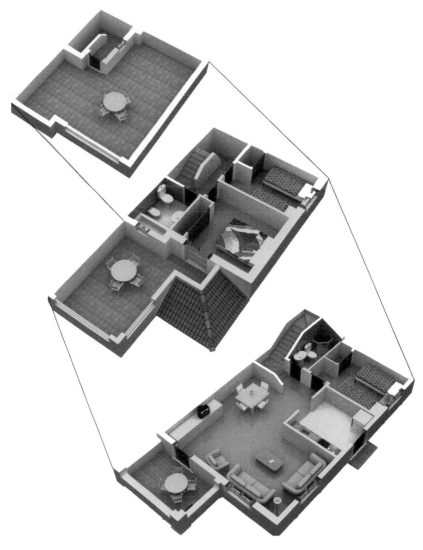

Fig. 5. Details of the property outlined in Appendix 1 and 2.

Traditional homes

Older Spanish properties exist. In most cases they have been modernised or rebuilt and called a reformed house. In the country they are called *fincas.* In the town they are simply town houses.

A reformed town house is in many respects an ideal property since it gives easy access to a town with the benefits of living in new, modern surroundings. Found in the narrow streets of small towns and villages, these properties have a number of cool, shady rooms. Built on a slope they often have several floors, balconies and internal courtyards invisible from the street.

But the classic is a *finca rustica,* located in the country. It is where dreams are made. It can be a labour of love, together with considerable skill, determination and money in order to rebuild an old crumbling building into an individual, personalised property of pride and charm. Renovating a property, or indeed maintaining it, demands very good DIY skills. Living in a rural location needs patience, tolerance and enthusiasm to deal with a lack of utility supplies.

New or resale?

Most people prefer to buy a new property. It can be good value. In some parts of Spain, an off-plan property is the only type available (see Figure 6 for an example of an off-plan apartment). It is rather like buying a car. Why buy secondhand if you can buy new? A resale property is slightly more expensive, after all the drives have been laid, gardens are mature and it often comes with furniture and fittings. A resale property built within the last ten years will still carry a guarantee.

Mention should be made at this stage of Spain's peculiar debt laws where the debt is on a property and not a person. Any outstanding property debt occurred by the previous owner is automatically carried over to a new owner. The complexities of this are explained later.

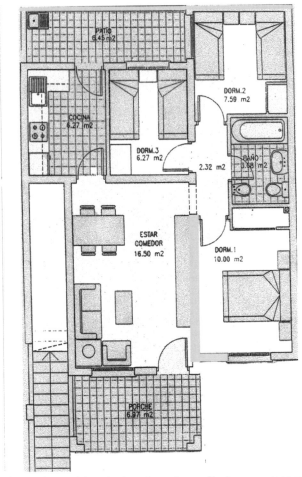

Fig. 6. An architect's drawing of an off-plan apartment.
The size of each room is specified.

WHICH DIRECTION?

There is a bay at Calpe with a hilly headland jutting out eastwards to sea.
Houses built on this hill face north. They are cold as they get little direct
sun. Individual houses, a terraced row, or apartments facing north all
suffer from the same fate – little sun in the winter months and

consequently cold interiors. These properties are sold not by referring to any direction, but by saying 'cool in summer'. For year round living it is better to choose a property facing south.

Or is it? Many Brits, starved of UK sun, usually want a property which faces south. They feel if they are going to move to the sun they must be in the sun. This can be wrong. Copy the Spanish, and let's face it, they have a lot of experience of living in the sun, and choose east-facing. If the main rooms of the property face the morning sun the living area will not be flooded with midday heat. An alternative would be to purchase a property with a westerly orientation. Enjoy the late afternoon sunshine and spectacular sunsets but once more the living area will never be subjected to direct midday sun.

A compass is a handy tool when viewing properties for direction is rarely stated in agents' literature. East, west or south but not north, for north-facing properties are the last to sell, often attracting discounts or special offers in order to complete the transaction.

MAGICAL HOUSING INGREDIENTS

What do we really want when buying a Spanish home? Is it a property close to the sea with easy access to the countryside, a town and an airport? Is it to be new, white, set in a large plot of land? Do restaurants, pubs, hospitals, doctors and dentists have to be close by? Are neighbours only to be British, Irish and the rather pleasant Dutch?

No, not really! What we do is to set a number of priorities, which are usually the price, the number of bedrooms, the type of house and the location. Then we look for position and character.

Position means location. Overlooking orange and lemon groves! Close to a pine filled ravine! At the edge of purple hills! Next to a marina! More simply it can be exotic gardens or a house that has obviously been well loved and cared for. Location is that little bit extra which makes a property highly desirable – and probably that little bit more expensive. It is no good buying a large detached property surrounded by cheap flats. It will just lose value. A property at the end of a street, facing a commercial centre will suffer the same fate. A property in the middle of a row of similar houses has nothing to commend it. Future resale values are dependent on the general ambience of the area.

Character is a personal thing, something that makes a property just that little bit different. Is it an individual detached property that has a number of unique features? How about porches, terraces for sitting in the sun and enjoying a glass of wine? Or a swimming pool perhaps? Large, white, airy rooms with walls covered in colourful pictures. Whatever it is, in the eye of the beholder it is that something special that makes a house a desirable home to live in.

WHAT DO PEOPLE REALLY BUY?

People moving to Spain for the first time often purchase a new property near the coast, sold by an international property company of some repute, giving a sense of security in a country where the customs and laws are unfamiliar to the purchaser. There may well be an 18-month wait for the property, which can be built to standard or individual design and is usually located on an urbanisation. This type of purchase is simple, with no debt issues to worry about. The property company is on hand to deal with any outstanding problems.

In many parts of the country a resale property is a common purchase. Slightly older properties in mature areas, where new buildings are not so prevalent, are an attractive proposition. Away from the concrete, the coastal hustle and bustle. People have in mind life in a rural town, or on an individual plot avoiding the disadvantages of an urbanisation. They seek to blend into Spain.

Discerning buyers look for something unique, something different. They are in the minority. They know the country well. They understand its culture, customs and procedures. They may have lived in Spain for a few years or may be buying a second house inland. Buying a plot of land, a ruin for renovation, or perhaps building your own, are all possibilities.

6

Finding the Money

*Some people overcome complexity by compromise,
achieving a 100% mortgage on a Spanish property, financing
it by a 50% mortgage extension on their UK property and a
50% Spanish mortgage.*

MORTGAGES AND LOANS

It is possible to borrow freely from outside Spain in any foreign currency for sums up to 1.5€ million without any authorisation provided the lender is not based in a 'tax haven'. A home-buyer in Spain can therefore obtain a mortgage from a lending institution in any country and in any currency denomination. In practice it is different. Lenders are always reluctant to lend against a property located in another country for it is difficult to repossess a foreign property if anything goes wrong.

However, lenders in Britain are quite relaxed about homeowners' equity in their UK homes being used to fund the purchase of a second property overseas. Most people who are looking to buy overseas have a lot of equity. As long as the repayments are affordable, extending a UK mortgage should not be a problem. In the majority of cases a UK mortgage will be in the same currency as the borrower is earning. It is easier to arrange than an overseas mortgage and the costs of remortgaging in the UK will be less than those involved in arranging an overseas mortgage.

The Spanish banks too can be mortgage providers. A Euro denominated mortgage is calculated on a different basis compared to charges on a UK sterling denominated mortgage. Spanish mortgage rates are commonly quoted as 'Euribor' plus a percentage. For example a mortgage advertisement will state 'Euribor + 1%'. Euribor is the Interbank lending rate used across the entire Euro zone. As such, it is used as a common benchmark for consumer borrowing across a wide range of loans including credit cards and mortgages.

There are no building societies or their equivalent in Spain with the exception of a few of UK parentage. Spanish banks therefore have a captive market for the provision of home finance. Spanish mortgages are on a repayment basis with loan and interest both repaid by instalments.

Endowment and interest-only mortgages are not known in Spain. The criteria for granting a Spanish mortgage are similar, but more restrictive than in the UK.

- The earnings of one or both purchasers are taken into account. Allowances are made for letting income.

- The property is valued not at market value, but at a rebuild cost per square metre. Most banks will not lend an amount whereby the monthly repayments are greater than 30% of net disposable income.

- The maximum mortgage for a non-resident is around 60% of the valuation and for a resident around 80%.

- A combination of a low valuation based on rebuilding cost and a low mortgage based on that valuation means an actual mortgage may only be 40% of the market value of the property.

- Mortgages are usually granted for a maximum of 15 years and repaid before age 75.

- A separate mortgage deed does not exist. The existence of a mortgage is stated in the *escritura* prepared by the *notario*.

- The cost of a new mortgage is around 5% and 1% for redemption. Life insurance for the amount borrowed is also required.

- Buying off plan with stage payments will only have a mortgage granted at final payment in the presence of the *notario* which means the size of the mortgage is also limited to the size of the final payment. As this can be 60% it is no problem. If the earlier stage payments are more substantial, banks will offer a credit facility for these payments.

If personal circumstances change, it may be necessary to raise money on a foreign property. The Spanish mortgage market is much less flexible than the UK's. Money is lent only in order to buy or improve a property.

Once the property has been purchased, equity release is virtually impossible. So the only way you can raise money on a foreign home is to sell it – and a forced sale is seldom on advantageous terms to the vendor.

However, financing a property in Spain can offer more options than a straightforward mortgage extension on a UK home. Less risk is achieved by borrowing in Euros. When currencies move, the asset will move in the same direction as the mortgage. Alternatively if income is in pounds, it is not a bad idea to have a loan in pounds as well, so any currency fluctuations will not change the payments.

Confused? Some people overcome complexity by compromise, achieving a 100% mortgage on a Spanish property, financing it by a 50% mortgage extension on their UK property and a 50% Spanish mortgage.

CASE STUDY

Purchasing with a mortgage

Question We visited Spain about one month ago and decided to buy a house. The agent was most insistent that we sign a contract and pay a deposit of 10% as other people were interested in the property. Before we signed the contract we explained to the agent that we required a mortgage in order to complete the purchase. He told us this was 'no problem' and arranged for us to meet a bank manager who informed us that he would be able to lend us 70% of the value of the property. As this was satisfactory for our purposes, we concluded our business and left for home.

Much to our surprise we were informed that the property we were purchasing at 200,000 Euros had been valued at 140,000 Euros and the bank was only prepared to loan us 98,000 Euros (70% of 140,000) compared to our expectation of 140,000 Euros (70% of

200,000). We now cannot afford to complete the purchase. What can we do?

Answer In order for the bank to issue a mortgage loan, they have to have the property valued and for this purpose they use a valuation company. It is normal for a valuation company to undervalue using a 'worst case scenario' instead of the current market value. It is unlikely that the bank will increase their percentage offer and equally unlikely that the valuation company will alter their assessment.

It is very important to obtain professional advice before signing any document and parting with any money. It is true that sometimes another person is interested in the same property, but this ploy is often used by agents to get a signature on a contract. Obviously the best course of action would have been to sign nothing until the mortgage situation was clear.

What is the position now? This can only be answered by reference to the contract. If the contract states that the deposit will be forfeited in the event of non-completion, then unfortunately that is the situation unless an amicable arrangement can be agreed with the agent and vendor.

It would have been possible to have a non-standard clause in the contract stating that a mortgage loan is required in order to complete the purchase, and in the event of this amount of finance not being forthcoming, the agent or vendor is obliged to give a full refund of the deposit. This situation is too late for that.

Obviously the matter can be discussed with the agent and vendor but it is definitely a 'sticky wicket'. A compromise solution with a refund of half the deposit, giving some compensation to the vendors, would seem a good idea.

NON-RESIDENTS' CERTIFICATE

A transaction to buy a Spanish property can be completed outside Spain. For example money could be transferred from a buyer's account in Edinburgh to a seller's account in Dublin. But to do this a Certificate of Non-Residence is required. It is issued in Spain by the Ministry of Interior and helps the Spanish tax man keep track of where the money comes from and goes to. This will take time; but without it a notary will not approve a property purchase.

TRANSFERRING MONEY

Regular transfers

The use of two accounts, one in a home country and one in Spain, should be enough for the transfer (*transferencia*) of money, pensions and day to day living expenses. The transfer of money between two accounts is straightforward irrespective of the currency involved but charges can vary and conversion from Sterling or Dollars into Euros is expensive.

Some people prefer to use three accounts: a UK Sterling account, a UK Euro account and a Spanish Euro account. Transfer Sterling to Euros in the UK, then transfer these Euros to Spain with instructions that all transfer charges are to be allocated to the UK account. The advantages of this may not be immediately apparent, but the benefits are avoidance of Spanish bank charges with the full identification of currency transfer costs, which is not always possible with only two accounts.

Offshore banking has some advantages for investments and tax free savings. Since Gibraltar, an offshore centre is so close to the Costa del Sol, it is still possible to bank offshore and live in Spain. Many offshore current accounts offer cash or credit withdrawal worldwide. However a charge of 2.25% taken from the exchange rate and 1.5% charge per withdrawal make offshore banking expensive. The benefits of offshore banking are now doubtful as the EU has closed tax avoidance loopholes by having offshore banks declare any interest earned to the tax authorities in the account holder's country of residence.

Any time money is transferred from a UK bank to an account in Spain a charge occurs. There are some exceptions but try to avoid paying a Sterling or Dollar cheque into a Spanish bank account. The charges are high – around 0.55% – and there is a 14 to 21 day delay while a cheque clears. A cheque from another country in the Euro zone suffers an even worse fate, taking six weeks to clear as there is no centralised bank clearing system. A normal cheque within Spain attracts a small charge but no delay.

To reduce bank charges always transfer money from outside Spain by electronic transfer. Always transfer Euros, not Sterling or Dollars. Always use a rapid bank transfer system such as SWIFT which assures the money is sent quickly. The charge will be a fixed fee of around £20 and 0.25% deducted from the official exchange rate from the UK bank and a further 0.25% from the Spanish bank. This deduction, in total 0.5%, can be paid by the sender or by the receiver, or split evenly which is the normal approach. European banks have introduced unique numbers for all bank accounts, incorporating a code for identity of the bank and branch involved as well as the account number of the individual customer. These are known as IBAN numbers. This, not name, address, sort code and account number should be quoted on all international currency transfers.

Specialist companies, competing with UK banks, exist for the regular transfer of money abroad.

A fixed monthly Euro requirement will vary as the exchange rate varies, so it is not possible to be exactly sure how much Sterling will be required to cover an overseas payment. Overseas payment plans allow the fixing of an exchange rate between Sterling and Euros for one year at a time. The monthly payments are collected from a UK bank by direct debit and transferred abroad on a set date each month. The costs of this service are an annual £50 fee and £7.50 per month, less than normal banking charges.

Large transfers

Transferring large amounts of money over a lengthy period of time from outside the Euro zone requires careful consideration. The variable exchange rate has to be taken into account. At its launch the Euro instantly revalued to 1.64€ against the Pound but in the aftermath of 9/11 moved to 1.39€. Which currency is weak or strong is a matter of conjecture. Either way, this swing of 18% is a major influence when large sums of money are transferred. It can take many months to purchase a property abroad, particularly in the case of a new development. It is therefore important to ensure protection from the volatility of exchange rates. This means that a property price quoted today is probably not the price eventually paid, especially in the event of staged payments when purchasing off-plan.

For example let us assume that you are UK resident buying a new villa in Spain. The developer will require a deposit in Euros immediately, then further stage payments during construction over the next 18 months and large payment upon completion. The price of the property is in Euros and this will not increase unless the specification is upgraded.

The actual cost in Sterling will be determined by the timing of the currency purchase. If the Pound strengthens during construction the cost will decline, but if the Euro strengthens costs will increase. To illustrate the potential volatility a property priced at 200,000€ would have cost £129,870 in January 2003 but increased by £12,980 to £142,850 by May (a 10% increase in just five months).

One transfer strategy would be to buy all the Euros now, thus fixing the cost at the outset. This is called buying currency for 'spot'. Deposit the bought currency to earn some interest and make payments to the developer as requested. Another transfer strategy would be to buy the Euros each time they are required to be sent to the developer. This means the purchaser has no idea what the final cost of the property may be.

A more complex transfer strategy, but one that is gaining in popularity, is to buy a 'forward contract'. In essence, a forward contract means buying the currency now, and paying for it when there is a need to make the individual stage payments. The requirement is to pay 10% now and a 90% balance upon the maturity of the contract. For example £50,000 worth of Euros bought now but not sent for three months means agreeing the rate now, placing £5,000 on deposit, and paying the remaining £45,000 balance in three months. If the exchange rate moves in the three-month period this will not affect the situation as the currency was bought at the originally agreed rate. It is possible to fix a rate on all forward requirements up to 18 months.

A forward contract can therefore remove the risk of exposure to currency fluctuations, which can occur between the time of agreeing a purchase and the completion of a purchase of an overseas property. However if sterling strengthens, it is possible to end up with an inferior exchange rate, lower than that on the open market at any point in time, but that is a risk each individual must assess and offset against the stability of a forward contract.

SPANISH BANKING

Banking in Spain is fragmented. There are about 150 different banks. They serve different markets having different functions. Clearing banks, savings banks, lending banks, cooperative banks and some foreign banks of French, German or British parentage compete with each other. These banks have many branches but naturally some of the smaller outlets do not offer a full range of services.

The Spanish banking system has some unusual procedures but it is efficient, usually staffed by friendly, hard working, multilingual people capable of offering a customer some of the most up to date services including telephone and internet banking. Credit or debit plastic cards are accepted for the purchase of consumer goods or for obtaining cash from an ATM (hole in the wall cash dispenser) of which there are many.

In selecting a Spanish bank it makes sense that some staff should speak English and have access to services such as mortgages and investments. It should be a main branch thus preventing delays in foreign transactions.

Bank accounts of residents and non-residents are distinguished separately with a non-resident account called *cuenta extranjera* and a cheque book (*talonario*) marked *cuenta en euros de no residente*. Different tax regulations apply but the banking operation for a non-resident account is exactly the same as for a resident account.

A current account (*cuenta corriente*) pays a low rate of interest – practically nothing (0.1%). A resident will have 15% of interest earnings withheld and paid to the Spanish tax authorities – less than practically nothing, and a non-resident should declare any liability to the tax authorities back home. Yet this account will incur some of the highest bank charges in Europe irrespective of the currency involved. Write a cheque and a charge occurs; transfer a payment and a charge occurs. With the exception of some free banking, charges occur every time a transaction takes place. Spanish banking is expensive!

Deposit accounts exist. They pay different rates of interest depending on the amount invested, the time period fixed in advance and the currency in which they are held. Again a resident will have 15% of the interest withheld by the bank to cover income tax. The bank gives a receipt which is deducted from income tax liability upon completing an annual tax return.

Free banking

The use of a credit or debit card on motorway tolls is free of charges. So too is a cash withdrawal from an ATM on a debit card provided it is within a bank's computerised system. There are two computer 'ring mains' in Spain – Servis Red and Tele Banco. All Spanish banks 'plug into' one or the other. It is not the brand of card that determines the charge but the computer system completing the transaction. Using the wrong one attracts a charge of up to 2€ per transaction. No other transaction is free unless you are receiving a pension from the Spanish state system.

Al Portador

Some tradesmen, among others, prefer a cheque (*talon*) made out to *Al Portador* (cash) as there is no record of who cashes it. It is a system of understating earnings for tax avoidance. Payment of services by this method usually 'forgets' *IVA* (VAT) from the charge so both parties benefit from the transaction. The use of personal cheques is less frequent in Spain than in most European countries. It is a country that prefers cash or credit cards. Post-dated cheques can be cashed immediately irrespective of the date and if a cheque is written with insufficient funds in the account, it is still possible to collect a partial amount up to the value of the available funds.

Bank statements

Anyone with a Spanish bank account will come across the practice of small, frequent statements. Monthly statements are not issued. After one or two transactions a statement is issued detailing any cash withdrawal, standing order or direct debit. A person with 12 normal transactions per month can expect four letters and probably ten to 14 slips of paper. A special account, for say a monthly mortgage payment, can expect two slips transferring money in and another two making the payment out. Do not be tempted to throw these slips away; in fact it is advisable to keep them all for at least two or three years as they often are the only receipt from a service provider. They are proof of payment for items such as car tax and are required for completion of an annual tax return (mortgage payments, bank fiscal statement and the payment of local taxes – *IBI*).

Letras

A *letra de cambio* is defined as a bill of exchange or a letter of credit (a written order directing a specified sum of money be paid to a specified person on a specified date) often used to make stage payments for a new house bought off-plan. This peculiarly Spanish practice is used for staggered payments, consequently a number of *letras* are made out. For example if a computer is purchased for 1,200€ it may be paid by signing 12 *letras*, of 100€ each, one to be paid each month. The seller will make out the *letras* with amount, date, buyers' bank, etc and they will be signed by the purchaser. The seller will send each *letra*, on the due date, direct to the purchasers' bank where it will be taken direct from the nominated account. Once signed, a *letra* is effectively cash. If the goods are faulty or if the *letras* are made out to the wrong person too bad! If a bank holds a *letra* then payment is expected irrespective of the circumstances.

Letras can be used as monthly stage payments for an off-plan property; usually one built by a Spanish builder, backed by a Spanish bank for typically Spanish apartments. A custom exists of purchasing other peoples' *letras*. For example a builder will sell all the *letras* to a bank or other institution at a discount in return for immediate cash.

Domiciling a payment

In other countries it is simply called a direct debit. In Spain it is called *domiciliacion de pagos* or the domiciling of payments where the word domicile means home. It is used to pay electricity, water or local tax bills. It is useful for non-residents who do not spend the whole year in Spain, ensuring services are not terminated for non-payment.

7

Meeting the People Involved

In some cases the agent operates on a fixed commission, but the following arrangement is more customary:
- *The agent asks the seller the price they wish for the property.*
- *They advertise and negotiate the sale of the property at another, higher price.*
- *The difference between the two prices is the agent's commission, which is rarely less than 10%.*

BUILDER

Looking at the amount of construction taking place in Spain one could be forgiven for thinking it is the country's major industry. Motorways are being built, distribution depots are springing up at major road junctions. Factories, assisted by EU grants, are being erected maintaining Spain's fast industrial growth.

In cities and along coastal strips hotels, apartments and houses continue to be built. Construction is big business. It is highly skilled. There is a shortage of skilled tradesmen, many travelling from the more remote parts of Spain to work on coastal developments.

What of the house builder? Broadly there are three types.

- A large builder accustomed to building 500 houses or one large apartment block per year. They may be in partnership with a developer but their main business preoccupation is with planning, finance and management. The actual building work is carried out by a team of site managers. The builder will rarely get involved in sales or marketing, appointing several multilingual agents to perform this task. Sometimes, however, they will sell direct to the public, cutting out agents and their commissions.

- A medium-sized builder constructing 30 to 50 units per year. A row of terraced houses or individually designed properties cut into the hillside are examples of the scale of the operation. The builder would be on site supervising the day-to-day activities but would also probably appoint an agent to carry out sales and marketing.

- A small builder, who may be Spanish or from Ireland, Britain or Germany, who will at the most be engaged in building a few individual houses per year, restoration work, or at an absolute minimum be engaged in laying garden patios or building dividing walls. They will carry out the work personally.

They are all highly skilled individuals. Starting work at 8 am and finishing at about 7 pm they will have breakfast at 10 am and a long break for lunch at 2 pm – complete with a customary bottle of red wine which will be taken, or left, much as a Northern European would treat a glass of water.

Bankruptcy policy

All builders should have an insurance policy to cover the possibility of going bankrupt before completing a property. The number and details of this policy should be stated in the purchase contract, but often is not, giving rise to the clear suspicion that insurance may not have been arranged.

It is desirable to have the security of this insurance policy, but there is always a need to be pragmatic. As an additional safeguard stage payments for a new property should be in line with building progress. After all, that is precisely the reason for stage payments.

Strangely it is small builders who are more likely to go bankrupt, despite their work being more tightly monitored by an owner. Larger builders have bank managers checking their cash flow. Look for a sign stating that a development is sponsored by a bank – this is an additional safeguard.

The financial consequences of a builder going bankrupt are clear. Time delays while an alternative builder is found also cause deep frustration.

Standard building specification

A modern Spanish house is built to a high specification with little wood used in its construction. It is a strong property, of concrete and brick, which tends to carry sound easily. This characteristic is at its worst in apartments, terraced and corner duplex constructions where sound travels easily through concrete floors. Water pipes are set unobtrusively in the walls which may cause problems should they leak. A major feature is low maintenance finish on both inside and outside walls. Houses in the southern part of the country are designed to achieve coolness in summer, partly through the use of window shutters to block out the hot summer sunlight.

Let's look at a typical, new property specification.

- Tiling in the kitchen and bathrooms from floor to ceiling.

- Ceramic floor tiles throughout the property.

- Brick masonry work with air gap insulation.

- Exterior low maintenance wall finish in cement roughcast or small marble chippings.

- Sloping roofs made with partitions forming the slope, ceramic bricks and cement mortar finish with curved roof tiles.

- Flat terraces fitted with ceramic terrace tiles.

- Shutters on windows.

- Interior walls to be finished in white, low maintenance plastic paint, known as Gotele style.

- Fitted kitchen units (top and bottom), worktops and stainless steel sink. Electric points for cooker, fan extractor, fridge and washing machine.

- Interior carpentry lacquered to natural colours with exterior door to 40 mm thickness and interior doors to 35 mm thickness.

- Copper plumbing installation with hot and cold. National sanitary fitments of a high standard.

- Sewerage pipes of PVC set in concrete.

- Reinforced foundations.

- Internal cabling for telephone and television.

Optional extras

Security

Security can be a problem. A property must be secure at all times, particularly when the owner is absent. The most effective method of securing a property is to fit metal grilles (*rejas*) to external doors and windows; they are available in many decorative designs. Alarm systems are available, usually linked to a central telephone control point in Madrid, but grilles are the most popular. This is not really an optional extra. For peace of mind it is a necessity.

Heating and air conditioning

Is heating, or air conditioning, or both, really necessary? The answer, as one would expect, depends on the exact area. Let us start with the Costa Blanca; after all it does carry that prestigious recommendation from the World Health Organisation. Portable gas fires, electric heaters or a wood burning stove to take the chill off a room, over a 12-week winter period, is all that is necessary. Similarly, fans to move the air around in summer will suffice. It has to be said, however, that more and more people are installing central heating and air conditioning as comfort levels are increased by an all-in-one system. Many new homes are built with this facility pre-installed.

Similar precautions for the Costa Blanca apply equally to the Costa del Sol, the Canaries and the Balearic Islands.

Moving north and inland a heating system is necessary. The centre of the country, including inland Andalusia, needs all the aids for comfortable living that can be mustered, with heating and air conditioning a necessity.

Swimming pool

With so many communal pools around, an individual private swimming pool is a luxury and not a necessity although it is rare to see a detached villa without one. A pool to cool off in the summer sun is certainly desirable. As an alternative, each small village has its own municipal pool. Water in Spain is precious. The unit cost increases with consumption, so pool owners pay hefty charges.

Garden

A garden completes a home. Residents should have a full garden laid out with palm trees and colourful hibiscus shrubs. Non-residents require a maintenance-free environment, laying out a garden to paving stones, chippings and the occasional water-thrifty shrub. Green lawns are rarely seen, such is the expense and difficulty of upkeep.

Additional charges

It may be necessary to purchase additional items for a new home such as:

- kitchen appliances, light fittings and bathroom fittings
- furniture, bedding and curtains.

AGENT

By virtue of their daily contacts, estate agents know who is buying and selling. Top agents keep files of buyers, sellers and properties. It is not unusual for a good agent, when they learn of a new listing, to sell it within 24 hours to a buyer they know will buy that type of property. An agent, given time and a detailed specification, will always find a property for a determined buyer. They may have to be chased occasionally, but that is part of the process of being determined.

The quality and integrity of estate agents has vastly improved in the last few years. Selling houses attracts some of the finest people. But the business still attracts some unscrupulous characters too, probably because it is possible to earn a handsome income without working too hard. Due to its financial structure the estate agency business opens doors to all types of people some of whom are not completely honest. However most agents aren't thieves and swindlers, if anything they're more honest than the average person because they have their reputations to protect.

Charges

Agents dealing in Spanish property often take high commissions. The lowest start at around 3% but the average is 10%. When selling a *finca* it can be 20%. How do they justify such exorbitant charges? Their answer is ambiguous, making reference to high advertising costs, commissions due in two countries and complex transactions involving different nationalities. In truth it is simply a seller's market with demand outstripping supply, causing many people to enter the lucrative business of house selling.

In the small, very popular town of Javea there are over 120 estate agents.

Why? With some house prices at 400,000 Euros plus, an agent only has to sell around ten properties a year to make an extremely comfortable living. It is often the case, in the final stages of house price negotiation, that the agent's commission itself may well be reviewed downwards. Very few agents in Spain operate on an exclusive basis and rarely expect to do so. It is quite common to find several agents selling the same property. Since their commissions may differ, so ironically may the house price.

Commission for selling a new house on behalf of a builder is usually around 10%. If a number of agents are selling the same properties they may compete with one another, discounting their commission by offering furniture packages and such like to prospective purchasers.

A different commission structure can operate for selling secondhand property, commonly termed a resale property. In some cases the agent operates on a fixed commission, but the following arrangement is very common:

- The agent asks the seller the price they wish for the property.

- They advertise and negotiate the sale of the property at another, higher price.

- The difference between the two prices is the agent's commission, which is rarely less than 10%.

This pricing structure can give rise to animosity. It is compounded when buyer and seller seldom meet, possibly creating an atmosphere of mistrust in relation to the commercial motives of the agent. An agent argues that if the seller gets the price they want and the buyer happily pays the asking price then everyone is happy. Or are they? For the commission structure breeds a system where:

- the buyer pays a high price

- the seller gets a low price

- the agent gains a high commission.

ABOGADO

What does an *abogado* do?

- Upon buying a property they will handle everything from drawing up the initial contract through to accompanying the purchaser and seller to the notary's office. They will check that nothing is wrong by making sure that there are no outstanding debts on the property and that non-standard clauses, designed to catch the unwary, do not appear in the contract.

- Where an off-plan purchase is involved they will check the contract and ensure stage payments are correct.

- They will act with a *Poder* (Power of Attorney) to buy and sell.

- They draw up wills and distribute the estate on death.

- An *abogado* does everything that a UK solicitor could do from divorce through to criminal proceedings.

Finding a good *abogado* is not an easy matter. They rarely advertise in newspapers. They have signs outside their offices, but these are discreet indicators of their presence rather than advertising mechanisms. It is word of mouth that results in the appointment of a good *abogado*. It may well be an agent who recommends an *abogado*. It could be the bank manager or a friend. Either way there are many people engaged in the highly respected profession of solicitor/lawyer who in Spain is called an *abogado*. They are admired for their ability to deal with Spanish law, where complex legal, procedural and administrative issues can bog down everyday affairs. It is best to deal with an *abogado* who speaks English well. In legal situations a working knowledge of the Spanish is not good enough.

Use a Spanish lawyer to help buy a Spanish property. Do not use a legal expert in your own country to check out the legal documents in another country. Would you use a German lawyer to check a British conveyance or vice versa? No. Why should it be different in Spain?

The relationship between an *abogado* and a notary (see later) needs some explanation. A notary will register a document provided it meets all the necessary legal criteria. They may even give some advice to the *abogado* on, for example, drawing up wills. But it is the *abogado* who will consider all the legal options for the client, draw up the documents to be registered and explain the legal 'ins and outs'.

It is important to remember that the appointment of an *abogado* is to protect a buyer. An agent is working for a seller. Let us be clear at the outset. The Spanish system of house conveyance is different. You are not dealing with solicitors who draw up and exchange contracts on completion. Remember the final lynch-pin of the Spanish system is the *notario*.

Power of attorney

This simple mechanism is useful if a purchaser cannot be in Spain when the legal paperwork requires completion. If the property is in joint names and one person cannot attend, then a Power of Attorney is essential. People on holiday can avoid weary queues at the *notario* by delegating a Power of Attorney to a legal representative.

A Special Power of Attorney can only deal with the buying or selling of property. A General Power of Attorney can deal with almost anything but is likely to embrace loans and mortgages.

To draw up a Power of Attorney, visit the local notary's office, with passport, and details of whom the Power of Attorney is 'for' and who it is given 'to', together with a small payment. A few days later the document will be ready for signature.

If a Power of Attorney is required it does make sense to have it drawn up at the onset of a purchase, but of course it is possible to conclude such an authorisation at any time. It is even possible to draw up a Power of Attorney without leaving home as the Spanish Consulate in any country can prepare one. Signing a Power of Attorney in a Spanish Consulate is the same as if it had been signed in Spain.

NOTARIO

A notary is a qualified *abogado* who has studied to become a notary. The public notary is an official who cannot be employed or instructed to act for an individual. The *notario* represents the State. They do not guarantee or verify statements or check contractual terms. They protect the interests of the individual by pointing out any pitfalls, by offering advice on legal points and volunteering information. Although some are bilingual, they are not expected to speak any language other than their native tongue or to explain the complexities of Spanish law.

A notary's main task is to make sure that documents are legalised, such as for a Power of Attorney, wills, certifying copies of passports, registering company charters, stamping the official minutes of a community of property owners, notarising a letter and most commonly, approving the deed of a property known as the *escritura*.

Most people meet the notary for the first time when concluding the purchase of a property. The *escritura* is signed and witnessed by the *notario* in the presence of the seller(s) and the purchaser(s) unless any party has utilised a Power of Attorney to excuse their own presence. The *notario's* duty is to:

- Check the name of the title holder and whether there are any charges or encumbrances against the property.

- Check the contents of the *escritura* and ensure it is read to the purchaser(s) prior to signing.

- Check that both parties have been advised of their legal obligations.

- Certify the *escritura* has been signed and the money paid.

- Warn parties if they knowingly undervalue the purchase price of a property by more than 20%, and ensure 5% of the purchase price is withheld and paid to the *hacienda* if a property is sold by a non-resident.

The end product of a visit to a *notario* is the *escritura*. It is a hardbacked copy of the property deed which is covered in official stamps, signatures and writing. Typed on thick, numbered paper, it is an impressive document produced to a standard format. All *escrituras* start with the date, the name of the *notario* and the protocol number which is effectively the filing references should another copy be required.

A meeting at the notary's office to sign an *escritura* can last about two hours. Just about everyone involved with the sale and purchase attends. The notary's office can on occasions get very crowded with many transactions taking place simultaneously. In some busy offices, dealing with a conveyor belt of new properties, the task is concluded simply with the builder's clerk (the seller), the *abogado* with a power of attorney and the notary themselves. A maximum of four people! But it is not always like this. With a resale property an agent, an *abogado*, a bank manager to give a mortgage and another to redeem a mortgage, joint sellers and joint buyers, the notary and their assistant can bring the total to ten people. Hopefully, someone can be a translator.

ASESOR FISCAL

For an ordinary resident or non-resident the *asesor fiscal* is someone who completes an annual income tax return to the *hacienda*. That is, unless the individual wishes to complete these tasks personally for there is no legal requirement to employ an *asesor fiscal*. Only a foreigner afflicted by the noon day sun would attempt to fill out tax forms and since taxes have to be assessed for everyone then by and large everyone has an *asesor fiscal*. A good one will always keep the client informed of tax regulations and legitimate ways of reducing any tax liability.

GESTOR

A *gestor* acts as an intermediary between Spanish officialdom and the general public, being a registered agent dealing with government departments. It says much about the Spanish way of life that such a person is necessary to deal with its bureaucracy.

They are competent, highly qualified administrators but what do they do? For the Spanish they simply deal with the complicated mass of paperwork. For foreigners they do the same, in a country where the language barrier, a new culture and complicated procedures cause additional problems. Some of the tasks covered by a *gestor* are:

* Application for *NIE* and residency.

* Gaining entry into the Spanish health system.

* Dealing with the payment of car tax, car transfer tax and other car related matters.

* Help in setting up new businesses.

A *gestor* does no more than a member of the public can do themselves but they do it for a number of people who have paid to have it done efficiently. Some people say, rather sheepishly, that a *gestor* is employed by people who have more money than time! But they know the ins and outs of the system and get the job done. State officials like a *gestor* too, as they know all the forms will be completed correctly.

OVERLAPPING ROLES

The role of an *abogado, asesor fiscal* and *gestor* can overlap. All can obtain an *NIE* and *residencia* (details in Chapter 11). In fact the first one visited will need an *NIE*. Whose door is knocked on first? Usually an *abogado*, as they are part of the property buying process. Like any good businessman, the *abogado* will seek to retain a future relationship with their clients after a property conveyance has been completed. There are taxes to be dealt with. Wills to be prepared and possibly a driving licence to be obtained. Entry into the medical system …

It certainly is convenient to have a one-stop-shop for all administrative, legal and fiscal affairs. Cost comes into it too, most people finding it better to use an *abogado* or an *asesor fiscal* or a *gestor* separately, as appropriate to the task.

AVOIDING PROBLEMS

Problems associated with purchasing a property abroad have been highlighted many times in the popular press. From a legal viewpoint Spain has not always been the safest place to buy. Most horror stories come at the start of the buying process. It is at the contract and deposit stage that things go wrong, where insufficient checks have been made, or inadequate procedures followed. Among the myriad problems experienced by buyers in Spain the most prominent are:

- Poor agents.

- A badly written contract.

- Properties bought without legal title.

- Issues surrounding developers and builders, lack of planning permission, companies going bankrupt, undischarged loans.

- An undischarged mortgage from the previous owner.

- An *escritura* which describes a property which has been altered to a degree bearing no resemblance to that described.

Who are the people who give rise to these horror stories? It is the British who trick the British, the Germans who trick the Germans and the Scandinavians who trick the Scandinavians and so on. Why? It is the language issue once again. Someone talking to you in your own language will sound more plausible, particularly someone who has already gained your confidence and understanding. It is unlikely that you would be tricked by someone of another nationality.

It cannot be emphasised too strongly that anyone planning to buy a property in Spain must take independent legal advice, in a language in which they are fluent, from a lawyer experienced in Spanish property law. Always deal with professionals and do not assume that because you may be dealing with a fellow countryman the advice is better, cheaper or even unbiased.

Do not sign anything, or pay a deposit, until you have sought legal advice. Once the advice is given – take it. Do not assume it is someone dotting Is and crossing the Ts. One of the most common phrases heard in Spain is about property buyers 'leaving their brains behind at the airport'. It is true! The rush to buy a dream home, or a pressurised selling trip, or even the euphoria of the moment often make people do incredibly stupid things, literally handing over cash deposits to agents or owners with little or no security.

While a conveyance procedure in some countries has one solicitor representing the buyer and another solicitor representing the seller, it is not necessary in Spain to have two *abogados*. It is accepted that only one is necessary, as a contract drawn up by an *abogado* can be assumed to be correct. After all, the final legal safeguard, a notary, is still to come. But herein lies a contradiction!

An agent selling a property normally appoints the *abogado*. They know the area, who is available and who they have worked with before. The contract may be perfectly legal but it is possible it will contain clauses more favourable to the seller than the buyer. If an *abogado* is dealing with hundreds of contracts on behalf of a builder or agent, where will their loyalties lie?

Conversely a person buying a property may be new to the district, probably does not know an *abogado* and can easily go along with this arrangement. But who pays the bill – the buyer. So it is wise for a buyer to appoint the *abogado* who draws up the contract, rather than the agent. If that is not practicable then a buyer should take additional independent legal advice from another *abogado* prior to signing the contract. So we are back to having two lawyers!

8

More Money Matters

It is quite common in Spain to have two purchase prices for a property. One price is the actual price paid exclusive of any fees or taxes. The other is a lower price declared in the escritura. The difference between the two prices is normally paid to the vendor in cash. It is a mechanism of tax evasion which if not radically abused, is tolerated by the Spanish tax man.

PROPERTY PRICES

Property prices will vary according to supply and demand, location, size and position. It is therefore not possible to give an authoritative price guide for all Spanish property. That is best obtained by referring to property magazines or specialist books on this subject.

As a guide, however, there is a 125 kilometre strip of coastline between Alicante and Cartagena which is developing at a prodigious rate. It is the southern end of the Costa Blanca and the newer Costa Calida both mentioned earlier. Properties there are heavily advertised across Europe and should be regarded as at the lower end of the popular price bracket. Not the lowest by any means, for Almeria, inland areas and the north of Spain are lower still. This is the area where property is selling fast; it is a price marker.

- 2 bedroom apartment   120,000 Euros
- 3 bedroom corner duplex   180,000 Euros
- 3 bedroom detached villa (standard)   280,000 Euros
- 3 bedroom detached villa (individually designed)   350,000 Euros

Using these benchmarks it is possible to make some additional generalised statements.

- Property is more expensive adjacent to the coast and cheaper 15 kilometres inland.
- Property is more expensive on the Costa del Sol, the Canary and Balearic Islands.
- Property is generally cheaper the further north you travel.
- Property in Andalusia, the home of white walled individual properties restored or in need of renovation, can be surprisingly expensive if only a short distance from the Costa del Sol.

- Within each region it is possible to find exclusive areas of new property attracting prices of 400,000 Euros and, conversely, close by in working towns cheaper property renovated to a high standard at around 200,000 Euros.

A national survey of property prices takes place annually showing the price of property regionally. The price quoted is the selling price of a property in Euros per square metre. These figures are also used to calculate property inflation. Property per square metre is consistently more expensive in Madrid and Barcelona and consistently cheaper in Galicia, Castilla La Mancha and Extremadura. However as the housing stock in big cities is predominantly tall apartments, and in the country rural town houses, comparisons per square metre can be misleading. The national average is around 1,500€ per square metre. For the last 20 years property inflation has averaged 18% per year.

PAYING THE MONEY

Stage payments for a new property purchased off-plan

Example 1	Example 2	Example 3
British developer	German developer	Spanish developer
10% reservation contract	40% on signing contract	3% reservation contract
40% stage payment	60% on completion	16% on signing contract
25% stage payment		14 *letras* each of 1.5%
25% on completion		60% on completion

In all three examples *IVA* is included in the price and paid at the various stages. The Spanish developer uses the peculiarly Spanish system of *letras*.

Payments for a resale property

5% to 10% on signing a contract
90% to 95% on completion
IVA – paid on completion

A partly built property

50% on signing a contract (walls, roof, windows and doors completed)
20% stage payment
20% on completion
10% retained for up to one year to cover snagging defects
IVA – paid on completion

The basic rules

All payments can be negotiated. Remember a contract is a private agreement between a buyer and a seller and cannot be overruled.

If the buyer fails to complete, deposits are non-returnable unless there is a clause in the contract to the contrary. If a seller fails to complete the transaction the buyer is recompensed to a value twice the amount of the deposit unless the contract states otherwise.

If a builder fails to deliver a new property on time penalty charges accrue. These should be stated in the contract.

Property sales between individuals follow a system of private contract and deposit(s), followed by the notary and final payment. There is nothing binding about this. If everyone agrees it is perfectly possible to go direct to the notary, pay the money and obtain the *escritura*.

ALLOWING FOR ADDITIONAL BUYING COSTS

It is normal to allow 10% of the property value declared in the *escritura* for the additional buying costs which covers three taxes, two fees and charges from an *abogado*.

Transfer Tax or *IVA* (Value Added Tax)	7%
Actos Juridicos Documentados on a new property only	1.0%
Plus Valia tax	0.5%
Notary fees	0.5%
Property registry fees	0.5%
Charges from an *abogado*	1.0%

Transfer Tax and *IVA*

Impuesto de Transmisiones Patrimoniales is the Spanish for Transfer Tax which is charged on a sale between two individuals. *IVA*, the Spanish equivalent of Value Added Tax, is a business charge on a sale between, say, a property company and an individual. Governments can vary taxes, and they do, but it is normal to allow 7% for either of these two taxes.

Actos Juridicos Documentados

Effectively stamp duty of 1% payable on a new property. It is not payable on a resale property.

Plus Valia tax

Plus Valia is payable on a resale property and a new property. It is assessed locally on an increase in the value of the land since the previous owner bought the property or a developer bought the land. An apartment on an urbanisation where little land is involved or where there has been no increase in value in a short time will result in a low *plus valia* tax charge. Conversely a home with a large plot of land, held by the previous owner for say 30 years, will suffer a high charge.

Of course it is the seller who should pay this tax. They have gained the benefit of the increase in land value. The law of the country supports this view. In practice however this tax has often fallen on the purchaser since it a more secure method of collection. After all, a vendor may flee the country leaving this tax unpaid.

A purchaser may feel, quite rightly, aggrieved at paying this tax. Recourse is simply to have a clause inserted in the contract stating it is the vendor who pays the *Plus Valia* tax and withholding this sum from the final payment.

Notary fees

These vary according to the value of the property declared in the *escritura* and the number of pages in the document. Allow 350 Euros or 0.5%.

Property registry

Again there is a fee to have the property registered. It is wise to allow 0.5%.

Charges from the *abogado*

Naturally this fee will depend on the amount of work done. If the basic paperwork has been handled to a straightforward conclusion then the charge will be low. If on the other hand there have been complications or the need to draw up multilingual contracts then the charges will be higher. Allow 1% for this charge.

Who pays?

The buyer and seller can agree between themselves who pays taxes, fees and charges. This can be incorporated into the contract and is not overridden by Spanish law. In practice however the buyer pays either directly, or on occasions indirectly when the agent incorporates these charges into an overall selling price. *Todos los gastos* is the Spanish phrase meaning all expenses arising.

It is also normal practice to deposit the approximate figure of 10% of the *escritura* value with the *abogado* or the bank manager (for mortgaged properties) who will pay these accounts on behalf of the buyer, submitting an itemised statement when transactions are complete.

Five per cent tax deposit

One last twist in the tail. If a property is bought from a non-resident, then 5% of the purchase price declared in the *escritura* must be deposited with the tax office in the vendor's name. In other words only 95% is paid direct to the vendor. Why? This deposit is designed to cover a non-resident's liability for capital gains tax.

BLACK MONEY

It is quite common in Spain to have two purchase prices for a property:

- One price is the actual price paid exclusive of any fees or taxes.

- The other is a lower price declared in the escritura.

- As a guideline, the difference between the two prices should be less than 15% to 20%.

- The difference between the two prices is normally paid to the vendor in cash.

This practice is known to agents, buyers and sellers, builders and developers, the *abogado*, the bank manager and the notary. It is known by the tax authorities. In fact it is known by everyone.

It is a mechanism of tax evasion which if not radically abused, is tolerated by the Spanish tax man. All taxes and fees are calculated on the value stated in the *escritura*, not the actual price paid. The Transfer Tax or *IVA* charged at 7% is effectually reduced to 5.6% if the *escritura* value is declared at 80% of true selling value. When reselling the same property a few years later a similar reduction needs to be applied to avoid excessive payment of capital gains tax as this too is based on a value declared in the *escritura*.

Many people are now seeing the folly of this practice but once started it is difficult to stop. The saving of, say, 1.4% in initial taxes on purchasing can easily be outweighed by a greater loss in capital gains on any profit

Almond blossom.

Fishing boats, Teneriffe.

Dawn, eastern Spain.

Cordoba.

Quenca.

Segovia.

Rice fields.

Street in Estellens.

Murcia cathedral.

Town houses and villas.

Mallorca.

made when reselling. If a low value is declared on purchase then the capital gains liability will be on a greater profit upon selling. It is in the interests of the buyer to declare the full value of the sale.

Spanish tax officers do not sit idly by. Renowned for being sharp but pragmatic, they maintain their own table of property values and are empowered to set a higher value which can result in an additional tax bill should they feel excessive tax avoidance has taken place. This scrutiny is mainly, but not exclusively, applied to a purchaser's tax liability. If they discover that the sale has been under-declared by more than 20% they can apply heavy penalties under the terms of Spain's *Ley de Tasas* which was enacted to prevent this practice.

'Black' is the term used to describe the difference between the actual price paid and the value declared in the *escritura*. 'Black money' describes a cash payment representing the difference in values. Incidentally the payment of 'black money' can also occur at the start of the buying process with an initial deposit paid as cash to the agent which in turn becomes their black money commission.

MINIMISING THE RISK

- Never pay a deposit direct to a seller. They may abscond. Never pay a deposit to an agent. They too may abscond. The agent will want the deposit paid to them in cash. But it is not their house! It is not their money. Ensure a deposit in placed in a bonded client account, from which it will not be released until the sale is final.

- Pay by cheque or a certified cheque or a banker's draft in Euros drawn from a Spanish bank account. Do not pay in cash.

- Never make a cheque out to an agent, only to a seller (reservation contract excepted).

- If the seller insists on anonymity ensure no money changes hands until at the notary – where a seller must be identified.

- Be fully aware if the deposit is returnable or non-returnable in the event of failing to complete a transaction. Alternatively ask the number of day's grace in which to change your mind.

- Do not accept a verbal agreement – ask to see it in writing.

- The payment of a deposit is the first financial and legal step in buying a property. It must be linked to a contract.

WHO SHOULD OWN IT?

There is more than one option when structuring ownership of a property. Each has advantages and disadvantages. The choice depends on personal circumstances, together with due consideration of inheritance tax liability. It is an important choice, for if incorrect, more tax will be paid than necessary both during a lifetime and on death. Inheritance tax consequences arise not only in Spain but back home too. (Inheritance tax is dealt with in Chapter 13.)

Joint ownership

This is the normal way of proceeding. Two people buying together will buy in both names. It gives a level of security. Upon death the other half passes to the fellow owner (UK inheritance law) and is taxed according to the relationship by Spanish inheritance laws. It is normal for the ownership split to be 50/50 but in the case of a second marriage with three children on one side and one child on the other the split can be 75/25, which would give a fairer distribution of inheritance.

Children named in the deed

In the example above, with two adults and four children, there is nothing wrong with having all six names on the deed in equal or unequal parts. If one person dies their share of the property passes equally to the other five. Spanish inheritance tax will be small, if anything. And the disadvantage – if the children fall out with the surviving spouse they could insist on a sale of the property unless an arrangement was constructed with the spouse retaining a life interest.

Property in children's names

In this case a property is in the names of the children only, with a life interest held by the named parents who paid for it in the first place. The property is the children's in whatever parts so defined. A life interest (*usufructo*) is the right to use the property for a lifetime. On the death of one person, the remaining spouse or partner who has a life interest would still be able to use it. On death there will be little or no inheritance tax. A disadvantage – the property is no longer owned by the purchaser and if families fall out, get divorced or children suddenly die it becomes complicated. As this is a peculiarly Spanish practice there is plenty of 'civil code' for guidance.

Off-shore company

A property may be owned by an offshore registered company, in a so-called tax haven, where the property is not in the name of the owner but in the name of a company. The owner of the company owns the property. When the property is sold, it is only company shares that are transferred. The same company continues to own the same Spanish property, so no

Spanish taxes are charged. But the company has a new owner.

A similar approach applies to inheritance tax – the company is bequeathed to an inheritor. The Spanish authorities, blocking this loophole, have placed a tax of 3% per annum on any property held by an offshore company. After three years it is cheaper to pay the taxes associated with purchase (10%) and after ten years probably better to allow for inheritance tax at 30%.

9

Understanding Legal Documents

The end product of a visit to the notario *is the* escritura. *It is a hardbacked copy, covered in official stamps, signatures and writing, typed on thick, numbered paper. It is an impressive document.*

All legal procedures and documents are important and failure to understand one may have serious consequences. Property documents can be broken down into four groupings.

1. Pre-purchase checks.

2. Signing a reservation contract or contract.

3. *Pre-escritura* for new properties.

4. *Escritura* and beyond.

All pre-purchase checks need to be completed before signing anything. Signing a contract signifies this has been done and everything is in order. An *escritura* merely legalises what has gone before. A contract, signed soon after the start of the buying process, is therefore the most important document in the property buying process (the most important documents are shown in Figure 7). A good contract, correctly worded, is of benefit to both the buyer and seller. Altering a contract is almost impossible. A bad contract creates unnecessary difficulties. Reneging on a contract involves losing a deposit.

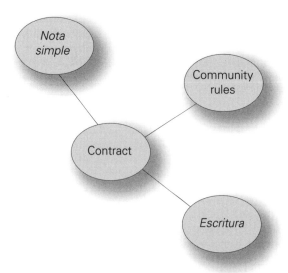

Fig. 7. The important legal documents.

PRE-PURCHASE CHECKS

An architect's drawing

It makes sense to have a plan of a house, particularly for a relatively new property or one bought off-plan (not yet built). What is required is neither a glossy brochure, nor a three-dimensional sketch or an artist's impression, but an architect's plan showing the dimensions of each floor and each room in square metres. For new properties this is a legal requirement with the living space in each room, the total build area and plot size all specified. The overall size of the property, again measured in square metres, determines its market price, its valuation for any mortgage, insurance premiums and an assessment for local taxes.

Plan Parcial

It also makes sense when buying land or a new property yet to be built, to have a line drawing locating the plot. This is called *Plan Parcial*, a Spanish term meaning a plan of parcels, or plots of land, which is registered with the planning department at the local town hall. It ensures land or property for sale is approved and registered with the town hall and secondly it shows other adjacent developments or roads planned close by. While a line drawing, supplied by the builder's architect will suffice on most occasions, a *Plan Parcial*, from the *urbanismo* at the *ayuntamiento* (town hall) is the only approved legal source. Prospective purchasers should also be aware of developments close to the sea which require to be approved by the *Jefatura de Costas* as well as the town hall.

Nota Simple

This very important document is often overlooked. Translated it means a Simple Note which is issued by the Land Registry Office and is a copy of the Property Registration details (see *Registro de la Propiedad* later in this chapter). For a property yet to be constructed, it is proof that the person selling is the registered owner of the land and that there are no debts on the land. For an existing property it shows details of the present owner, if the property has an outstanding mortgage or loan, or if it has any debts registered against it.

Obtaining a copy of the *Nota Simple* is straightforward. First locate the registry office with jurisdiction over the property or land. This is not always in the nearest town or village. Secondly complete a request for information form and pay a small fee, then return in a few days to collect the *Nota Simple*.

Establishing the right to sell

While the *Nota Simple* will give ownership details of an existing title, it makes sense that further documents are requested to establish the person selling has the right to do so. Details in the *escritura*, passport or *residencia* number and *Certificado de Empadronamiento* should all agree with the facts in the *Nota Simple*. If not there is something wrong. An examination of property dimensions recorded in the *escritura* should also be the same as the actual property – if not an illegal alteration has taken place.

Quota of community charges

Buying a property in Spain, particularly on an urbanisation or in an apartment block, invariably means becoming a member of a community of property owners. A country property or a town house in a street will not have to deal with community issues.

It is advisable to at least understand approximate community costs involved prior to signing a contract, but in most situations this would not materialistically affect a buying decision. Indeed, with a very new project an overall community budget will not have been determined. Conversely with an established community the costs, constitution, chairman and committee members will all be established.

The allocation of costs will vary. On an urbanisation of 1,000 homes of equal size each will carry a charge of 0.1% of total expenditure. If however the urbanisation had 500 large and 500 small homes the allocation could be 0.125% and 0.075% respectively. This allocation of costs, called a quota and expressed as a percentage of total community costs, is determined at a very early stage in any new development. The information should be available upon signing a contract.

Debts

Spain's laws carry any debt on a property over to the new owner. Prior to signing the contract a check has to be made to ensure there are no encumbrances such as mortgages, or outstanding debts such as local taxes or community charges, and all service bills have been paid in full. A mortgage or loan is repaid at the notary. The following is a process for checking this:

- A copy of the *Nota Simple* will tell if there are any mortgages or loans against the property. A seller is not trusted to pay off a mortgage on their own accord, so it must be paid at the time of signing the *escritura*.

- Enquire at the town hall to check any unpaid local taxes: *Impuesto Sobre Bienes Inmuebles* (*IBI*).

- Enquire through the Community of Owners, or their management company, to ascertain all community charges have been paid.

- Check receipts provided by the seller that all bills for electricity, water and telephone have been paid.

A first-time buyer probably does not have time or local knowledge to carry out these checks. An agent should do this, but often does not. A notary will carry out some of these checks. An *abogado* will do a fine job as their professional reputation is at risk. But a bank manager issuing a mortgage will do it even better since the bank's money is at risk. Remember, all unpaid debts on a property are inherited by the buyer.

Impuesto Sobre Bienes Inmuebles (IBI) and valor catastral

An *IBI* receipt is not available for a new property, but is available from the town hall for a resale property. The *IBI* receipt will show the property's *catastral* reference number and the *valor catastral*, the official assessed value used in calculating *IBI*. The assessed value is usually substantially less than the real market value.

The *catastro* is a second system of property registration, defining the location, physical description and boundaries of a property which unlike the Property Registry concentrates on ownership and title. Both systems should of course agree. What is in the *escritura* should be in the *catastro certificate*. Sometimes the boundaries of a property, or even the property itself, can differ because people have accepted descriptions made in one document but not in the other.

Although the certificate comes in two parts, one is a description in words and the other a plan or photo. A clerk at the efficient *SUMA* offices (where they exist) should find all relevant details on a computer, avoiding the inevitable form-filling, cost and delay.

SIGNING THE CONTRACT

Reservation contract

This document, sometimes referred to as a pre-contract, represents the first step in the buying process for a new property – a property bought off-plan. It will usually necessitate the payment of a non-returnable reservation fee, which is included in the initial deposit. It is an outline agreement to reserve the property and should contain as minimum the following details.

- Name, address and passport number of the purchaser.
- Name, address and the business or personal identification of the agent or developer or both.
- House type, plot number and address of the property.
- The price in Euros. This should clearly state if *IVA* (Value Added Tax) is included in the price.
- The reservation deposit and payment formulae.
- Date and signature of both parties.

Purchase contract

A purchase contract is the most important document in the Spanish property buying process. It will repeat information in a pre-contract adding greater detail. Signing a contract signifies the following:

- The plan of the house and location of the plot are satisfactory.
- The *Nota Simple* has been checked, is in order and the person selling has the right to do so.
- The contract has been read and understood.

- Signing the contract triggers the payment of usually a non-returnable deposit.

- The purchaser has the necessary monies, or mortgage, available to complete the transaction.

A contract should be well written and comprehensive. It is normally in Spanish but on some occasions can be set out paragraph by paragraph in Spanish and the mother tongue of the purchaser, ensuring no ambiguity. The key points are:

- It reconfirms all previous details, namely the parties to the agreement; the ownership of the land, its registration and freedom from debts; details of the plot; the size and description of the property. The seller, not an estate agent handling the deal, is the owner of the property.

- It sets out in detail the method, dates, currency, price and payment schedule; financial penalties for failing to complete and any charges for connecting water and electricity.

- Where appropriate, confirms a purchaser respects the obligations of law surrounding the Community of Owners and gives details of a nominated district court should things go wrong.

- Sets out any special clauses such as 'subject to obtaining a mortgage'.

Two types of purchase contract

A full preliminary contract (*contrato privado de compraventa*) is the most common type of document. It is called a private contract because it is freely agreed between the buyer and seller in the presence of an *abogado*. It is an agreement to commit both parties. The seller must sell and the buyer must buy subject to the conditions they agree.

An option to buy contract should be avoided. This is a written document in which the seller agrees to take a stated property off the market for a fixed period and to sell it at a stated price to a stated person at anytime within a stated period. It lacks definition, is a standard form completed by an agent and not checked by an *abogado*.

PRE-ESCRITURA – FOR NEW PROPERTIES

Certificado Final de la Direccion de la Obra

Translated this simply means Certificate of the Termination of the Building. It does not mean the building is falling down, quite the opposite in fact. It is a certificate produced by the architect when a new house is finally complete. It enables a declaration of a new building to be made at the notary's office and is used to obtain the *Licencia de Primera Ocupacion* detailed below.

Licencia de Primera Ocupacion

The Licence of First Occupation is obtained from the town hall on production of the *Cerificado Final de la Direction de la Obra*. It is a licence to inhabit the property, registers it for the purpose of local taxes and the connection of services. The electrical supply company will not connect to an unregistered property.

On new developments the initial supply of water from external pipes and electricity without meters is often obtained from a builder's supply point. The reason for this is simple. The completion and occupation of property is faster than the ability of utility companies to connect their supplies.

Building insurance

A new property will be insured by a builder during construction and at a low nominal value for 12 months from the date of occupation. A copy of this policy should be available, stating the insured value and what exactly covered. When a house is occupied, a top-up building policy is all that is required for the first year. It is obviously sound practice to have an additional household insurance protecting against damage or theft and against claims by others. This is important if a property is empty for a long period – such as holiday homes.

ESCRITURA AND BEYOND

The end product of a visit to the *notario* is the *escritura*. It is a hardbacked copy, covered in official stamps, signatures and writing, typed on thick, numbered paper. It is an impressive document produced to a standard format. All *escrituras* start with the date, the name of the notary and the *protocal* number which is effectively the filing reference should another copy be required. The *escritura* is the deed for a property. It is a record of the property at a point in time.

There are three versions of the *escritura*. The *Copia Simple* (not to be confused with *Nota Simple*) is a copy of the *escritura*, less the signatures which is sufficient to prove ownership. It is available on the day of signing at the notary and is recognised as suitable for most legal purposes. It is normal for the purchaser to hold a copy of this document.

The *Escritura de Compraventa* is the main document signed in the notary's office. The *Escritura Publica* is the *Escritura de Compraventa*, complete with its many official stamps from the property register which converts it into a public document.

An authorised *abogado*, the property owner, or in the case of a mortgage the bank, can hold the *escritura*, but irrespective of who holds it someone has to collect the finished document from the notary. Thousands of *escrituras* lie gathering dust in notaries' offices, uncollected or unregistered because of some minor technicality. In the latter case the property will remain unregistered until the 'problem' has been rectified.

The document itself is written in legalised Spanish making literal translation almost impossible. The owner never holds the original deed, only the first authorised copy. The original is held at the notary's office. A second authorised copy can be requested in the event of the first being lost.

No one can doubt the necessity of having a comprehensive document, particularly one which clearly states debts or mortgages, or indeed the transparency of having this document made public. But there is considerable ceremony associated with its preparation and signing which many people believe to be unnecessary. It certainly legalises a situation but it does not alter or undo anything that may have been agreed previously at the contract stage.

Registro de la Propiedad

This is the last piece of paper in the buying cycle. Strangely it is not the *Escritura Publica* that is the final step, as it is registered with the property register being over-stamped *Registro de la Propiedad*. This simple one-page document simply closes the loop to the *Nota Simple* which was considered at the start of the buying cycle. What does all this mean? The *registro de la propiedad* registers the property in a public place giving details of who has the title, which notary was responsible for the *escritura* and lists details of any mortgage or loan.

Licencia de obras

Although a property has been built to a correct specification, let us assume there is a need to make a small modification such as building a dividing wall between an adjacent property and perhaps a shed to hold some tools.

Do you need permission to do this? The answer is yes. In fact permission is usually quite straightforward. A visit to the town hall, the completion of a paper entitled *solicitud de licencia de obras*, clearly marked '*minor*', and the payment of a small fee, will result in the necessary approval. That is of course provided the modification fits in with the overall urbanisation design, style and specification.

FAST-TRACK CONVEYANCE

A fast-track conveyance is a situation prevalent in the southern end of the Costa Blanca and Costa Calida where the whole infrastructure is devoted to marketing new property yet to be constructed – buying off-plan. Here procedures involving the purchase of new properties have been speeded-up. A fast-track conveyance is different from the standard procedure where time is important and no one wishes to be held up waiting for legal matters to be completed. Purchasers wish to move into their holiday home immediately. So the final payment is made direct to the builder, possession taken immediately, and the parties to the purchase sort out the paperwork (*escritura*) at a later date; usually by a power of attorney.

CASE STUDY

Don't get mugged

New owner	I expect there will be long queues at the bank? *Firma* here, *firma* there, that sort of thing?
Agent	Probably Senor, probably. Are you aware that 7% of the total payment is cash for the builder?
New owner	No.
Agent	You are now!
New owner	Let me understand this. This house cost 100,000 Euros. Today's final payment of 25% is 25,000 Euros of which 7,000 Euros are cash and 18,000 Euros are a banker's draft.
Agent	Yes, that's how things are done here. By the way the house costs 93,000 Euros. Do you understand? This will benefit you too. Less tax to pay! (He taps his nose twice with the index finger of the right hand.)
New owner	Presumably this transaction is known to the appropriate authorities?
Agent	Si, Senor, everyone knows. (The money is collected and placed in a black briefcase.)
Agent	Let us go Senor, to pay the builder. We do not want to get mugged!

So to the builder, with a banker's draft and a bundle of black money. The builder's clerk is a young woman who wears standard black, tight, flared trousers associated with smart business attire. She smiles in a tired sort of way, exhibiting years of experience as she carefully counts the money.

> *Clerk*   *No para mi* (not for me).
>
> The task is completed and she smiles again. A key is pressed on a word processor and a document is produced which translated states that the full price for the property has been paid. Ambiguity par excellence!
>
> *Clerk*   Here are your keys and receipt.
>   *Buena suerte* (good luck).
>
> She smiles for the third time in a kindly way.

BUYING WITHOUT AN *ESCRITURA*

There are situations where a property can be purchased without an *escritura* for perfectly legitimate reasons. However, this is not a permanent situation.

A common situation arises when a *Nota Simple* states the property is owned by 'Heirs of Senor ...' or the owners of rural land are brothers and sisters whose family has owned the land for years without a written document. A solution for property with no registered title is to obtain from the property registry a 'negative certificate' which means the registry has no recorded owner of the property. The buyer requests the property be registered in their name and the seller justifies their title by any documentary evidence possible. The proceedings are published in case anyone wishes to protest. If not, in one year, the *escritura* is finalised.

A more complex process, involving investigation and court action, is called the *Expediente de Dominio*, which is used to establish a title when a property is registered, but in the name of a person who no longer claims it, perhaps because the original owner has died. The claim is published and evidence taken to a court for a ruling on ownership.

Yet another reason for buying without an *escritura* is holding an off-plan property on a private contract. In this case a purchaser buys a partly built property on a private contract from a developer and sells it on at a profit before completion thus avoiding taxes. In a fast moving property market, where properties are bought for investment, they can change hands quickly and are not registered. Investors wait for the next buyer to come along and complete in the normal way. Owning a property on a private contract without an *escritura* means a property cannot be seized by a court in order to pay a debt, it avoids taxes and conceals an asset from any interested parties.

AUTHOR'S NOTE

Readers may wish to turn to the first five Appendices of this book detailed below.

1. A purchase contract issued by a builder for a new property.

2. Community rules.

3. *Escritura.*

4. A purchase contract drawn up by an *abogado.*

5. An option contract signed on behalf of a client by an agent.

The first three appendices are for the same property. Further examples of contracts are highlighted in Appendices 4 and 5. The first is extremely well written by an *abogado* for an unusual property. The other, for a resale property, is designed only to benefit the agent's receipt of black money.

A good contract – Appendix 4

The contract itself is written in a similar manner to a final *escritura*. It is clear and unambiguous. No black money is involved. Let us look at some of the interesting contents.

- Urban dwelling, in a state of ruin, situated in (full address), comprising ground floor with room and corral, occupying 40 square metres.

- Mortgage in favour of (bank) for 27,000 Euros.

- Also to the account of the seller will be the charges derived from the cancellation of the mortgage as well as the work of amplification of the *escritura*.

This old property is situated on the edge of a Spanish town. It was a home to a family and some animals. The owner took out a mortgage to renovate the property into a modern town house with a high building specification. He then sold it. The cost of an architect to specify the new building dimensions for inclusion in the *escritura* was the responsibility of the seller.

A bad contract – Appendix 5

The brevity of this contract hides a number of important commercial issues. But first the background. This is the resale of a relatively new holiday home by a multilingual Scandinavian agent, his clients largely UK-based.

The contract states the agent acts in representation of the seller. In fact no signed document existed between the agent and seller. The agent could have taken the deposit and simply vanished. He did not have the right to sell the property.

The fixed agreed price of Euros is even more misleading. It does not state what is included in the price. In fact the price did include all legal fees, taxes and the agent's commission. The net figure after these deductions is the money received by the seller. But this figure is not stated in the contract. Since the value in the *escritura* is also less than the value in the contract, black money involved goes direct to the agent.

The contract deviously hides all key commercial figures. The largest and most important is the agent's commission.

A buyer should always take legal advice. In this case nothing untoward occurred since both the buyer and seller were honourable people. The agent was not dishonest, but unquestionably sharp.

10

Doing It Yourself

Do not purchase a picturesque, tumbledown farmhouse only to discover that renovation is way beyond personal skills and means, or get hopelessly bogged down trying to get planning permission to satisfy all the requirements of building regulations.

Foreigners predominantly purchase a new home bought off-plan, or a resale home. There are however other combinations.

1 Picking a plot of land and model property design from an agent, developer or builder.

2 Renovating a ruin – the classic rural finca.

3 Going it alone, building it yourself, on rural land.

Building or redeveloping a home is not something to be taken lightly. It is not a case of buying land, approving a design, appointing a builder, going away and maintaining telephone contact. There is a need to be personally involved or, failing that, to ensure the project is managed by a local architect or building engineer. Before starting on a project of this scale appoint a good *abogado*, one who can recommend a builder and an architect who can also assist with the building permit and planning application.

PLOT OF LAND WITH A MODEL PROPERTY

There is little difference between this approach and buying a standard property off-plan. A plot of land is chosen from a plan and a house type is selected from several options available from a builder – type A, or type B, etc. With some thought and attention to detail a dream house is possible but personal supervision of the building programme is absolutely necessary – location of the plot, position of the property on the plot and adherence to the building specification.

RENOVATED HOUSES

Many people like the idea of returning a derelict ruin to its former glory. Restoration is less popular than building new, because it is usually more expensive and there are limited opportunities to acquire a cheap, suitable shell building. Do not purchase a picturesque, tumbledown farmhouse only to discover that renovation is way beyond personal skills and means. Either that, or get hopelessly bogged down trying to get planning permission to satisfy all the requirements of building regulations. It is all too easy to become entangled in red tape if not conversant with Spanish laws, or not speaking Spanish fluently.

Whatever the condition of the building, the process starts with the purchase of a resale property. It may be run down. It may even be a ruin. It is probably in the country but can be a terraced house in a Spanish town.

Since the external structure of the building will probably be altered, a number of checks need to be carried out before purchasing. The most obvious is to check with the planning department at the town hall to find out exactly what can be done. Demolish, rebuild, extend upwards or outwards, or simply renovate, are the options. With a town house, renovation and an upward extension are probably the only possibilities.

In the country do not assume anything is possible. In fact the height, size and number of properties per 1,000 or 10,000 or 30,000 square metres is regulated by a town hall planning department and it may only be possible to extend the footprint of a property by a small amount. Ten thousand square metres of land is a normal requirement for *rustica* properties (country land with no building designation and a water supply) and 30,000 square metres for land without a water supply.

Check utility supplies. If none, how much will it cost to install them? Important questions need answering about supply of electric, supply of water and sewerage disposal, TV reception, telephone and communication systems.

In the UK it is normal to have a building survey on a property prior to exchange of contracts. Some UK surveyors operate in Spain providing a survey to cover all structural elements, such as the roof, walls, doors, windows, floors, outbuildings, and garden walls, external and internal decorative state. Damp tests will be carried out by an electronic damp meter to each room in the house, and comments made on general services such as water, electricity, gas supply and drainage.

Not many people use a surveyor in Spain. A Spanish surveyor costs around 1,000€ plus additional translation costs. People embarking on a building project normally have enough confidence in their structural knowledge to trust their own judgment and those who don't should not be embarking on such a large project in the first place.

Assuming all these checks are satisfactory it is now safe to purchase the property and proceed to the next step of obtaining a *licencia de obra* (building licence) from the local town hall.

PURCHASING LAND

Before purchasing urban or rural land a number of vital enquiries have to be made. Most important is the planning status attached to it which may prevent development. For example it may be designated an area of beauty or designated for a specific purpose only. With areas of outstanding beauty, retaining natural charm is often a key issue with planning departments. Asking planning authorities to change this designation is difficult. On the other hand planning applications are almost automatic where an area has been approved for urbanisation or general housing development.

Look for a town plan called the *Plan General de Ordenacion Urbana* (*PGOU*), the municipal building plan. Drawing it up involves both local and regional government, with the latter not always approving the usually overambitious plans of the former. It involves political, social and legal considerations. A town plan is not a static document. It can involve strategic planning and detailed consideration of individual planning applications. Looking at a plan is one thing, understanding it is another, more complex issue, with specialist help often necessary.

The purchase of rural land has further complications. Where are the boundaries? Are there any rights over the land? What can it be used for? All these factors have to be checked before proceeding. While the boundaries may be marked by paint on rocks, numbers, or metal stakes in the ground, this is useless if a defining piece of paper contradicts these markers.

Lastly where crops and trees are growing, or land is used for agricultural purposes, check the water rights. Check the road access for winter rain. Are there any tracks or rights of way across the land? Are there any building developments or roads planned close by? Will the property be overlooked by any high development obstructing the line of sight? Do adjoining neighbours have any prior purchasing rights?

Buying land is much the same as buying a house. It needs a contract and an *escritura* and a visit to the notary. It requires the payment of *IVA* which in the case of land is 16% (remember it is only 7% for a property). It also requires pre-purchase checks and the one check that nearly always ends in some discussion is boundaries of rural land since they are often described in vague terms. If problems exist with boundaries an official surveyor can survey and measure the land thus identifying its boundaries and size. The findings form part of a new *escritura*. Thereafter the way to proceed is to compare the *escritura* (assuming one exists) with the *catastro* certificate (a map with boundaries). There is a need to have officially recognised boundaries and a statement of the exact square metres in both documents. While they may not agree initially, this can be corrected upon purchase when a new *escritura* and a new *catastro* description are brought in line.

All done and correct? It is now safe to purchase the land and proceed to the next step of obtaining a *licencia de obra* (building licence) from the local town hall.

BUILDING LICENCE – NEW AND RENOVATED PROPERTIES

Officially titled *licencia de obra* – a building licence – this document can also be called a building permit or *permiso de obra*. It is necessary to have a building licence to build a property on a piece of land in the country or in the town. It is also necessary for renovating an older property.

Previous checks at the town hall will have given an assurance that there is no objection in principle to being issued with a building licence, which is the equivalent of planning permission. When discussions take place the issue of local building codes will arise. The distance between the boundary and any other building? The distance between a wall and a road? The number of storeys? What about already established urbanisation approval?

It is necessary to understand the applicable building codes before submitting final plans. It may be that approval of building licences can be influenced. A Spaniard accompanied by a local architect and builder known to the town hall planning people will gain maximum flexibility from the codes. Foreigners, who are often accustomed to obtaining planning permission for as little as a garden shed, like to keep to the rules but find the whole planning system wearisome and unless accompanied by a local architect or Spanish solicitor they are unlikely to be able to grapple with the issues involved. To obtain the required building licence, a detailed set of plans with a building specification, called a *memoria*, must be submitted for approval.

Delay often accompanies the final issue of a building licence. It is a point of no return for local authorities. Final approval may be referred to *Provincial* or *Comunidad* level if the project involves a change from *rustica* to *urbano* designation, or the district does not have an approved *Plan General de Ordenacion Urbana* (*PGOU*). Building licences come more quickly when renovating a ruin than when building new – a ruin is unsightly and in the eyes of the planners best upgraded. Lastly, one person frequently called to assist a private person is the local mayor. Remember they usually want the project to succeed and, of course, a personal vote.

Do you really need an architect?

There are two main ways to obtain a *memoria*. One method is to go to a local builder who will have a stock of house types which can be altered to individual requirements. The second method is to have plans drawn up by an independent architect, local or from anywhere in the EU, in line with individual tastes and requirements.

A good architect can match financial limitations to budget, sort out muddled thinking, design a home and steer a project through the planning stages. The best way to find a good architect is by personal recommendation. Find one who has worked on a similar project, where examples of their work can be seen and references obtained.

Pressure exists for the appointment of architects. It reduces the number of unsightly designs and removes some responsibility from the town hall. In fact architects' drawings are necessary to obtain a building permit and an architect signs off the completed building. The minimum architect's fee is set by their *Colegio de Arquitectos* at 6% of estimated construction cost. However, as is the way in Spain, the estimated cost of construction will be reduced by around 20% in all official documents. The actual construction cost will be around 75% of the finished market value. An *aparejador* (building engineer) supervises building construction on the architect's behalf with a charge of 1.5% of estimated construction cost.

If it goes wrong

Builders often say 'you can build anything you want here. If it goes wrong we will pay the fine.' Don't believe it! The statement may be accurate, it may be made with the best of intentions, but it is not correct or contractually binding. Some people deliberately build without permission. If the town hall does not object within seven years it is approved. If permission has not been granted, or an alteration has breached planning rules, a fine of 5% of the alteration value is imposed, provided the modification is deemed satisfactory and can be legalised. Blatant breeches incur a fine of 20% and demolition of the building.

Development deals

Along the Mediterranean building is taking place at a prodigious rate. In some popular areas planning authorities have special deals with a developer where land is re-zoned to permit greater building in exchange for part of a developer's profits to increase the town's revenue. This does raise a few eyebrows, especially where a mayor or councillors have an interest in the land, but it is not illegal. The best that can be said is that the extra income assists all residents in reducing taxes.

MEMORIA

The architect prepares a *memoria de calidades* (building specification). While many items such as concrete, bricks and electrical wiring are standard, many are not. Roof tiles, floor tiles, wall tiles! Electrical fittings, bathroom fittings and kitchen fittings! Doors and windows! Getting the *memoria* correct is important as a builder uses it to prepare a competitive quotation. Any changes or extras made later will cost more, usually a lot more, as they are no longer competing.

If a builder fails to meet a building specification they are accountable in law. The *Ley de Ordenacion de Edificacion* makes a builder legally responsible for ten years for any damage resulting from foundations, load-bearing walls and other structural elements. They are responsible for three years for damage caused by construction material defects, and one year for the external finish. An architect is also responsible for ten years for incorrect instructions and undetected defects in the land such as subsidence.

BUILDER

The *memoria*, used as a basis for quotation, should also be incorporated into a building contract as a basis for payment. The largest fee should be paid on completion and the smallest fee paid up front. A building contract should be similar in style to a contract for an off-plan property stating what is included, method of payment and a definite completion date with penalties for late completion. Like a purchase contract this is a key document, not to be considered lightly and should be checked first by an *abogado*.

The balance of an architect, an *aparejador*, a *memoria* and a building contract all checked by an *abogado* should give total safeguard to anyone going it alone. An alternative to all this is just to let the builders in or build it yourself. You know exactly what you want, are confident of costs and specification. This is not recommended, but when renovating a town house with little or no external modifications, it is often done.

Many people think they can take shortcuts. Never mind the rules. Who do they meet? A cowboy: someone who offers services in return for a sum of cash, then either disappears, or carries out such horrendous work that the client ends up spending more to rectify the damage.

In the UK many of these cowboys are named and shamed on television. Trading standards officers investigate and some are prosecuted for the slipshod work they do, or for overcharging customers. But what about Spain, where there is a lack of effective trading standards control? In almost all the cases, a victim has paid thousands of Euros to have building work carried out, before realising they are being taken for a ride. They meet with aggression from the people who carried out the work. 'Try and sue me, this is Spain and you won't get anywhere'.

In a lot of cases, people prefer to put the experience down to bad luck rather than pursue the matter through the courts. In some cases they realise they have appointed a builder without due care and attention. Very few pursue the matter through the courts, partly through their own embarrassment and the possibility of throwing good money after bad.

To avoid this go by the rules, but if absolutely determined to appoint a builder for a small job, check the credentials of the person being considered. If they are a registered builder they will be able to show valid *IVA* documentation. Secondly, any good builder will show work they have previously done and allow an independent conversation with their clients so that their credentials are verified. Beware of hidden extras because there should not be any. If changes take place to a specification they should be by mutual agreement and be included on an amendment sheet to the contract. And lastly, at no time pay large sums of cash up front.

FINAL STEPS

Once the building is complete we are back to the procedures outlined in the previous chapter, starting with the *Certificado Final de la Direccion de la Obra* and the *Licencia de Primera Ocupacion* through to the notary and the *Escritura*.

CHARGES AND BUILDING COSTS

Fees and legal costs

Land survey	0.5%
Architect	6% (calculated on an artificially low building cost)
Building engineer	1.5% (calculated on an artificially low building cost)
Building licence	2% (4% of material cost)
Legal costs, including *IVA*	10% to 19% (remember *IVA* on land purchase is 16%)
TOTAL	20% to 29%

Building costs

- A good specification for construction work (a reformed property) – 750€ per square metre.

- A good specification for construction work (a new detached
  property) – 1,500€ per square metre.

Payments to a builder

20% on signing the contract

20% on completion of walls and roof

20% on completion of inside

10% for outside work – walls, patio, pool

10% retained for up to one year to cover defects

IVA – paid on completion or in stages

11

Settling In

There is more water consumed per head of population in Spain than in any other European country ... most of this is used in agriculture, leaving drinking water in some coastal areas both scarce and impure.

MOVING IN

After the waiting and, if new build, some inevitable delays, it is time to move in. There is a lot of work to be done. Moving house at the best of times is stressful, moving to Spain – either to a holiday home or permanent one – is both exciting and hard work.

In practical terms you need to carry out a series of tasks in a focused, planned and methodical way. Agents offer some assistance at this difficult moving-in stage and this can be very helpful. The first few days in a foreign country, making decisions with different customs and procedures, can be disconcerting. Help from a knowledgeable person is very welcome, speeding up the process by going to the correct place, at the correct time.

VIEWING A NEW PROPERTY FOR THE FIRST TIME

Having probably seen a show house, some brochures, a plan and location diagram, the viewing of your own completely new house for the first time is approached with considerable enthusiasm. It is there where it should be. White walls with ochre coloured window frames are set against a clear blue sky. Inside the walls too are white, contrasting with the dark orange bathroom tiles. A bidet too! The bedrooms are large, spacious with fitted wardrobes. Yes, it's exactly what you specified.

On the other hand roads may not be finished, water and electricity are still to be supplied by the builder through outside pipes and cables, the garden is non-existent and the house needs a good clean.

The emotion and pleasure of seeing a new home for the first time need to be quickly replaced with a more measured approach. In a new home, even with a ten-year guarantee, some faults are inevitable.

If any major faults exist, immediately stop the purchasing process until they are rectified. Go back home if need be, but on no account make the final payment. This of course is an unlikely scenario, after all the building has been inspected by the architect, but to be realistic major faults can and do happen. Time for talking it may be, but this is time for action too and is best achieved by the purchaser refusing to complete the transaction.

Draw up a list of minor faults (known as a snagging list) and give it to the builder. Rectifying building faults is a wearisome process at the best of times and in Spain it is no better. Delays, procrastination and battling with *manana* will result in considerable frustration, but remember it is Spain, where time is not important, so constant friendly pressure will be necessary to sort out faults.

EQUIPPING A HOUSE

As an alternative to moving furniture from back home, items can be purchased in Spain. Furniture packages to equip an entire property are readily available. They come in different sizes, style and quality. The range goes from a package for a simple two-bedroom holiday home to a large expensive package for permanent living, in a distinctive, colourful, Spanish style.

Price and service is the key when purchasing these packages. Is the supplier recommended? Are the goods in stock? Can they be delivered in a few days? It is easy to give and take an order, but with so many items in a package it is important to have a guaranteed delivery time for them all.

ORGANISING UTILITY SUPPLIES

Moving house means there are always practical things to do such as organising telephones, electricity, gas, water, insurance and all the other things which are part of everyday life.

Telephone

Telefonica, the Spanish telephone company, is a major communication organisation within European. It has a good reputation for service and efficiency with consumer prices similar to other countries. The installation of a new land line or transfer of ownership of an existing land line present few problems. Mobile phone technology is as advanced as anywhere in Europe; internet and broadband connection are freely available.

Electricity

Iberdrola is the Spanish electricity supply company. It is usual to have disruptions to supply. Power cuts are a fact of life. They can last for a few minutes or several hours. Power supply is also different. Firstly all homes have circuit breakers which can trip if there is a power surge. Secondly, plugs are of a Spanish configuration and lastly all light fittings have screw-in bulbs.

Gas

Gas supply is by bottles, or by exception on urbanisations from a central supply point. Two companies operate nationally with gas the cheapest way to cook and heat water.

When you purchase a resale property you should inherit gas bottles on which a legal deposit has already been made. Supply of gas is by a door to door delivery service, exchanging an empty bottle for a newly filled one. Alternatively take the bottle to the nearest depot for exchange.

The purchase of a new property having gas water heating or cooking requires a contract to be signed for a gas bottle supply. The property is inspected to ensure it is well ventilated and safe for gas. Once the contract has been signed, full gas bottles are supplied for a fee. They are exchanged when empty for full ones at around 10€ each. The same result can be achieved by going to the local market, buying a couple of empty bottles and then exchanging for full ones in the normal way.

Water

There is more water consumed per head of population in Spain than in any other European country. This is a remarkable statistic. However, most of this is used in agriculture, leaving drinking water in some coastal areas both scarce and impure. Very little water is wasted. Desalination plants are commonplace as political masters of towns and cities seek to increase supply.

Insurance

Household insurance is not difficult to arrange as there are many British and Spanish companies which advertise in English language newspapers available throughout coastal areas. Insurance costs are low compared to other parts of Europe.

CUTTING RED TAPE

Spain has a reputation for red tape and bureaucracy which has its origins in duplicated decentralised government. At local level, small 'stand alone' administrative offices deal with everyday aspects of Spanish life. Little co-ordination takes place. During this settling in period a number of administrative tasks need to be undertaken. The best way to accomplish these is to assemble all the necessary pieces of paper and decide who is going to do it – you personally, or a *gestor*.

Tourist or resident?

It is well known that British people, and for that matter foreigners from Northern Europe living in various Mediterranean locations, are not clearly defined by their own social perception of tourist, seasonal resident, temporary resident or permanent resident. The law is quite clear, irrespective of property ownership and taxation.

- Up to six months' stay, a person is a non-resident.

- Over six months' stay a person is a resident.

Many Northern Europeans live permanently in Spain without a *residencia* and without paying taxes – they are illegal immigrants with only their passports protecting them from greater legal penalties. Why do they do it?

Perhaps the answer lies in a reluctance to grapple with red tape in changing status, or perhaps they are reluctant to break the ties from home. Are they seeking to vanish from various authorities or hoping to escape taxation? Are they ignorant of the facts? There are no benefits in maintaining a tourist status if resident more than 183 days in Spain – only the risk of a fine. A person who lives in Spain more than 183 days, whether or not holding a *residencia*, becomes liable to pay Spanish income tax.

In fact the Spanish tax system is geared to provide greater tax relief to residents rather than non-residents by reducing capital gains tax, not having 5% of the price withheld when selling a property pending a review of capital gains liabilities, and a reduction in inheritance tax, *renta* tax and income tax.

Tourist status

The EU allows free movement in its member states for all its citizens, provided they have a national identity card or a passport. The UK is one of the few countries in Europe which does not issue an ID card but this may change. Until it does, a valid passport is required for UK citizens to enter Spain and for internal identification purposes thereafter.

A further 90-day extension called a *permanencia* can be obtained once per calendar year, so with this extension it is possible to stay as a 'tourist' for a total of six months. To apply for a *permanencia,* which is stamped in the passport, go to the foreign department of the nearest police station with a passport, two photos, and some evidence of your ability to finance a stay in Spain for a further 90 days. The *permanencia* is a little used procedure, but it

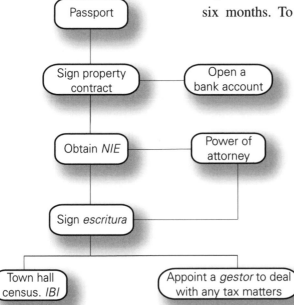

Fig. 8. Non-residents'/holiday home owners' decision tree

technically bridges the gap between a 90-day short-term stay and permanent residence over 180 days. A tourist is a person who spends fewer than six months in Spain in one calendar year.

A tourist may own a home, and many do, but anyone who stays more than six months must apply for a *residencia*. Figure 8 shows the steps a tourist must take in Spain when purchasing a home.

Fiscal identification number

All residents or non-residents with financial dealings in Spain must have an identification number. It is called *Numero Identificacion de Extranjero* (*NIE*), the significant word *Extranjero* meaning foreigner. *Numero de Identificacion Fiscal* (*NIF*) is the equivalent for Spaniards which in their case serves as a fiscal, identity and passport number.

To get an *NIE* go to the foreign department of a police station with a passport plus one copy, two passport photographs and complete the relevant form provided. Foreigners will quickly become accustomed to a way of life dependent on personal identification by an *NIE* number. An *NIE* is required for:

- Purchase of a property, a car and other expensive items.

- Dealing with the tax authorities.

- Identification on other documents such as insurance policies or bank records.

Permanent status – *residencia*

Intending to live permanently or to spend more than six months each year in Spain? Then no later than 90 days after arriving, begin the process of applying for a *residencia* (this is effectively an identity card). To do this, again visit the foreign department at the police station with the following documents.

- Copy of valid passport and *NIE* number.

- Three passport size colour photographs.

- The completed form.

At the police station finger prints are taken. In about six months a plastic *residencia* card is issued. It's a new identity in Spain, renewable every five years. The passport goes into the file at home to be used for

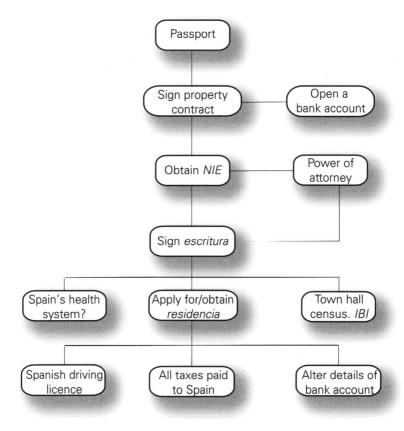

Fig. 9. Residents' decision tree.

international travelling only. Obtaining a *residencia* also necessitates a visit to the bank to change account numbers and alter the cheque book from non-resident to resident. It also means paying income tax to Spain rather than to a 'home' country and altering driving licence details. Figure 9 shows the steps a resident must take in Spain when purchasing a home.

Signing on the *padron*

A foreigner's first encounter with the *ayuntamiento* (town hall – see Figure 10 for a review of its roles) will probably be to register as a new resident of the town.

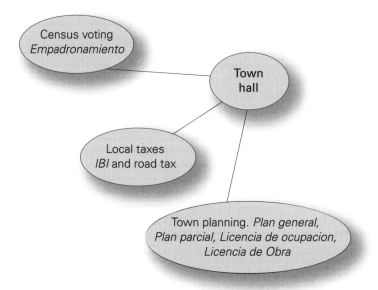

Fig. 10. Role of the town hall.

- Visit the town hall with a passport and evidence of residing in the town (*copia simple* or *escritura* or *residencia*).
- Complete some details. Provided more than six months each year is

spent residing in the municipality and the individual is not registered in another municipality at the same time, they will now be on the census of inhabitants residing in the area administered by that *ayuntamiento*.

- An *Empadronamiento Certificate* (census registration certificate) is issued.

Not everyone wishes to vote. Who are the candidates? What do they stand for? An EU citizen signing on the *padron* is entitled to vote in local elections and can be elected to office. They can also vote for their local European parliamentary representative or again stand for office. One per cent of foreigners in coastal regions have been elected to the well paid job of local councillor. The only additional qualification is to speak Spanish.

The more people registered on the *padron*, the greater amount of funds received from regional government.

Collecting *IBI* (*Impuesto Sobre Bienes Inmuebles*)

One role of the town hall is to collect local taxes. This operational role detracts from its political and management role and as a consequence collection has been subcontracted in some provinces to a third party. *Gestion Tributaria Diputacion de Alicante*, known as *SUMA*, undertakes this for the province of Alicante. *SUMA* manages local taxes authorised by town halls, provincial councils and other public organisations from most of the 140 municipalities that form Alicante province. They are responsible for collecting *IBI* (*Impuesto Sobre Bienes Inmuebles* – a local tax based on property value), *IVTM* (motor vehicle tax), a tax for rubbish collection and any other local taxes.

IBI is a local tax, rather like rates/poll tax/council tax in the UK but at a fraction of the cost. The services offered by a municipality are considerably less than in the UK. Home owners may have to take their rubbish to a central collection point. Street cleaners are rarely evident. Social services exist, but only to a limited degree. An *IBI* bill for a town house may only be 100€ per year reflecting a level of service, a degree of central funding and, more importantly, an artificially low level of property valuation. However this has to be balanced against community charges for a private development which can be as high as 1,500€ per annum reflecting shared costs for roads, pools, gardens and lifts.

Assessment of *IBI* is based on the fiscal value (*valor catastral*) of a property. The *IBI* tax rate is 0.3% for agricultural properties (*rusticas*) and 0.5% for urban properties (*urbana*). However, provincial capitals, towns with over 5,000 inhabitants and towns providing special services can increase the rate to up to 1.7%. To calculate an *IBI* bill multiply the fiscal value by the tax rate. A property with a fiscal value of 25,000€ in a village with a tax rate of 0.5% will have an *IBI* bill of 125€ per year.

Medical treatment

EU residents visiting Spain can take advantage of health care agreements providing their home country has a reciprocal agreement with Spain. The UK does. EU residents should apply for a European Health Insurance Card (EHIC), (which has replaced form E111), on line (www.ehic.org.uk) or by phone (0845 606 2030) three weeks before planning to travel. You can also pick up an application form from a post office. EHIC is normally valid for three to five years.

Temporary health cover administered through EHIC is not an acceptable solution for Spain's new permanent residents. It is of course possible to take out medical insurance, which is one way of dealing with this issue.

Emergencies, visits to the doctor and hospital are normally covered by such a policy but medicines and dental treatment are not.

Public health benefits, under the Spanish state health scheme called *INSALUD* (*Instituto Nacional de la Salud*), include general and specialist medical care, hospitalisation, laboratory services, medicines, maternity and some dental care. Anyone who pays regular social security contributions to *INSALUD* by virtue of their employment is entitled, for themselves and family, to free medical treatment.

Free entry into the scheme is allowed for:

- EU residents holding a *residencia* who are in receipt of a state pension and are over 60 (female) or 65 (male).

- A dependant of someone (wife or husband) can also enter the scheme provided they are both residents of Spain. For example a man not yet 65, who is married to a wife who is 60, is regarded as a dependant and both are entitled to enter the scheme.

- EU nationals, resident in Spain, who are disabled or receive invalidly benefit.

- EU nationals of retirement age, but not in receipt of a pension, may be entitled to health benefits.

This is the procedure to obtain a *Tarjeta de Sanitaria* (Health Card):

- Obtain form E121 from the Social Security office back home.

- Assemble a *residencia* (or proof of application), a passport and a copy, and *NIE*.

- Go to the appropriate Social Security office to complete some paperwork.

- Follow directions which will lead the applicant to a nominated medical centre which will allocate a doctor.

Emergency medical services in most EU countries, including Spain, are good. In a life-threatening emergency call for an ambulance and mention the nature of the emergency. Telephone numbers, which can vary from province to province, are in the phone book, near the start, under the heading *Servicos de Urgencia*. Ambulances come under the umbrella of social security ambulances, Red Cross ambulances or 24-hour private medical centre ambulances. They are equipped with emergency equipment and staff trained to provide first-aid. The ambulance service is usually free.

Driving licence (*Permiso de Conducir*)

A tourist visiting Spain and driving either their own car or a Spanish rental car can do so with a licence issued in their home country. An international licence also issued in their home country would be better as the standard format can be more easily identified by authorities.

Since 1996 a Spanish resident from another EU country can drive in Spain with their original, home country licence for as long as it is valid, with no obligation to take out a Spanish licence. However if the holder is a resident in Spain and not opting to obtain a Spanish driving licence, it is still legally necessary to present their UK licence to the *Jefatura Provincial de Trafico* for its details to be entered on their computer.

However the licence has an old address and for a new resident of Spain it is better to exchange it for a Spanish driving licence. If anything goes wrong it makes life just that little bit easier. It can reduce problems at roadside checks.

To exchange a UK licence for a Spanish licence:

* Go to the information counter at the provincial traffic department

(*Jefatura Provincial de Trafico*) with the UK licence.

- Complete an appropriate form (*Solicitud de Carnet del Permiso de Conducir*) and present a residency card, a photocopy, the old driving licence and three passport style photographs.

- The new licence is not for life. It is renewable every few years according to age: every five years for those aged 45 to 70 years and every two years for those over 70 years. An embarrassingly simple medical examination is necessary, which is carried out at an approved centre, lasts one and a half minutes and costs 35€.

Since 2004 holders of EU photo card driving licences can drive legally in Spain without the need to register or exchange that licence. If the licence bears a previous UK address, drivers should always carry proof of their residence in Spain when they have lived in the country for more than six months.

12

Understanding Personal Taxation

Since we have difficulties with tax at the best of times, a new resident or non-resident grappling with the language of tax authorities has little chance of getting a declaration correct. Enter the asesor fiscal *who will not only perform these administrative tasks but may even suggest legitimate methods of tax avoidance.*

INTRODUCTION

Spain is no longer the tax haven it once was when taxes were low and tax evasion a way of life. Today it is more difficult to avoid paying taxes and penalties are severe. However, despite the efforts of the authorities to curb tax dodgers, tax evasion is still widespread. Many non-resident homeowners and foreign residents think they should be exempt from Spanish taxes. Some inhabit a twilight world and are not officially resident in any country. Yet tax evasion is illegal. It is a criminal offence with offenders heavily fined or even imprisoned. On the other hand, tax avoidance, paying as little tax as possible and finding loopholes in the tax laws, is common. It is not so much the level of taxes, but the number of different taxes, sometimes for small amounts, which makes taxation complex.

Personal taxation

- Income tax (*impuesto sobre la renta de las personas fisicas*) is payable by residents on world-wide income and by non-residents on income arising in Spain.

- Non-residents and residents with more than one property must pay a property income tax (*rentimientos del capital inmobiliario*), which is usually referred to as *renta*.

- Wealth tax (*impuesto sobre el patrimonio*) is payable by residents and non-residents on high-value capital assets, including property.

- Capital gains tax (*impuesto sobre incremento de patrimonio de la renta de un bien inmueble*) is payable by both residents and non-residents on the profits made on the sale of property and other assets located in Spain.

- Inheritance and gift tax (*impuesto sobre sucesiones y donaciones*) is payable by residents on the transfer of worldwide assets and by non-residents on Spanish assets, upon death (see Chapter 13).

Other taxes

- Property tax (*impuesto sobre bienes inmeubles – IBI*) is paid by all property owners to the town hall, whether resident or non-resident.

- Taxes concerned with buying a property, including transfer tax (*derechos reales*) and land tax (*plus valia*).

- Offshore company tax (*impuesto especial*) is an annual tax on offshore companies that does not declare an individual owner of the property, or a source of investment.

- Waste collection (*basura*) is an annual tax payable in some areas, whether resident or non-resident.

- Motor vehicle tax (*impuesto de circulacion*) is paid annually by all those owning a Spanish registered vehicle together with a one-off registration tax upon purchase.

PRINCIPAL FACTS

Taxation is at the best of times complicated. In that context the Spanish taxman does not disappoint. As you would expect, the tax system is also ever changing. Most taxes in Spain are based on self-assessment where the individual is liable to report and calculate any tax due. The *Agenda Estatal de Administración Tributaria* collects government taxes but it is commonly called by its old name, *Hacienda*. The Spanish tax year is 1 January to 31 December. Tax returns must be presented between 1 May and the 20 June. Tax is paid at the same time as its declaration in June, or 60% with the balance by the following November. Tax returns are submitted to the district office where a person is resident for tax purposes, or they can be filed and payment made at designated banks. Payment must be made in cash as personal cheques are not accepted, although if filing at a bank where an account is held, they will make a transfer to the tax authorities – the preferred method. If no payment is due on a declaration, it still must be filed at the tax office in the normal way. Delay in filing a tax return may result in a surcharge while late payment of a tax bill will result in a surcharge of 20%. Copies of tax returns should be retained for five years.

Since we have difficulties with tax at the best of times, a new resident or non-resident grappling with the language of tax authorities has little chance of getting a declaration correct. Enter the *asesor fiscal* who will not only perform these administrative tasks but may even suggest legitimate methods of tax avoidance. It is not necessary to have a fiscal representative but fiscal representation is cheap, about 70€ per year for one person. For the relatively small cost involved, most people are usually better off employing a fiscal representative to handle their tax affairs rather than doing it themselves. For anyone owning more than one property, or a commercial property, or a foreign company owning a property in Spain it is legally necessary to have a fiscal representative.

It is possible to obtain free tax advice from the information section at the local tax office where staff will answer queries and assist in completing a tax declaration via their PADRE computer system. Some offices have staff who speak English and other foreign languages. An alternative is to present details direct to a bank that in many cases has PADRE forms on its computer. Most *asesor fiscals* use the PADRE program as well.

A non-resident spends less than six months per year in Spain. A Spanish resident is one who spends more than six months per year in the country, who has a *residencia* and has notified the tax authorities back home of their departure on form P85. This triggers entry into the Spanish tax system, which has a treaty with other European countries designed to ensure income which has already been taxed in one country is not taxed again in another country. Spanish residents are taxed on their worldwide income, whereas non-residents are taxed in Spain on income arising in Spain, which is exempt from tax in their home country.

There are two important points – firstly there is a five-year limitation on the collection of back taxes. If no action has been taken during this period to collect unpaid tax, it cannot be collected. Secondly, UK government pensions are taxed in the UK and not in Spain.

To complete tax returns, some documentation is necessary.

- Personal details; *NIE*, *residencia* number, address, age and marital status.

- Proof of income.

- A year-end bank statement showing any interest received and average balance. The interest is added to income and the average balance is part of the worldwide assets for wealth tax.

- A recent *IBI* receipt which will contain a property value (*valor catastral*) which is used to calculate *renta* tax.

- Receipts for tax paid in another country.

- Details of any changes in stocks, shares, investments or insurance policies.

- Details of any changes in major assets such as property, boats and artifacts.

- Proof to claim any deductions.

INCOME TAX

It is not necessary to file a tax return if income is less then 8,000€ a year. This applies to married couples and retired people too. The only condition – no more than 1,600€ of this income is from investments. A salaried worker earning less than 22,000€ probably does not need to make a tax declaration. This does not mean non-payment of income tax. It means that their withholding tax, taken out of their salary during the year, has been carefully calculated to match their liability. The tax office recalculates their final tax bill and makes any refund.

There are four steps to determine tax liability:

1 Calculate gross income.

2 Deduct allowances.

3 Apply tax rates.

4 Deduct further allowances.

Calculating gross income

Income tax is payable on both earned and unearned income. Taxable income includes salaries, fees, pensions and capital gains for residents, letting income, dividends and interest payments. It also includes employee benefits such as profit sharing plans, bonuses, company car, payment in kind, stock options and children's private education. And of course for a non-resident or a resident with more than one property it also includes *renta* (see later).

Deducting allowances

- All social security payments.

- A personal allowance.

- A deduction from income – a wage earner allowance.

- An allowance if unemployed and accepting a job in different locality.

- A disability allowance.

- A dependant's allowance.

- Professional and trade union fees.

- Spanish company pension contributions.

- A percentage of an annuity.

- Child-support payments made as a result of a court decision.

- Maintenance payments as the result of a court order.

- Legal expenses.

- Sixty per cent of any dividends.

Applying tax rates

Income tax rates for individuals start at 15% on taxable income up to 4,000€ and rise to 45% on taxable income above 45,000€. Tax payments are allocated between the Spanish state (85%) and the autonomous regions (15%), although some autonomous regions, e.g. the Basque Country, Catalonia and La Rioja, offer reductions in their apportionment. The table overleaf demonstrates the combined tax payable.

Taxable income €	Tax rate %	Cumulative tax €
Up to 4,000	15	600
4,000 to 13,800	24	2,952
13,800 to 25,800	28	6,312
25,800 to 45,000	37	13,416
Over 45,000	45	

Deducting further allowances

After calculating gross income, applying deductions, calculating tax due from the percentage table above and before arriving at a final tax bill, certain other deductions can be made. They have a dramatic effect on a tax bill as they are applied on a net figure.

• Personal income tax paid in another country against the double taxation treaty.

• 15% of the cost of the purchase or renovation of a principal residence but excluding additions such as a garage, swimming pool or normal maintenance.

• Deductions for mortgage payments – capital plus interest.

• 20% of the value of donations to charities.

• 15% of the amount invested in a mortgage savings account.

• 10% of life premiums or premiums for an invalidity policy.

• 75% of any *plus vaila* tax paid as a result of a property sale.

Example

Let's focus on a retired couple now resident in Spain. They have owned their property for a few years and have carried out no alterations during the current tax year. She has a state pension from the UK. He has earnings of 29,200€ from various sources but mainly occupational pension schemes and investments. Income tax liability is simple to calculate.

She pays no tax at all and is not required to make a declaration as her earnings are under 8,000€ per year.

He will have a personal allowance of 3,400€ deducted from gross income (4,200€ if over 65 years). Taxable income of 25,800€ at 28% will result in a tax bill of 6,312€ as there are no further deductions or allowances.

RENTA

A property owner's tax on deemed letting income (*rendimientos del capital inmobiliario*) is usually referred to as *renta*. *Renta* is nothing to do with renting out a property and nothing to do with *IBI* either.

All non-resident property owners or residents owning more than one property in Spain are deemed to receive an income of 2% of the fiscal value (*valor castral*) of their property or 1.1% if the fiscal value has been revised since 1 January 1994. Non-residents pay a flat rate tax of 25% on this income. A property valued at 100,000€, at a tax rate of 1.1%, will have a liability of 275€. It should be noted that the valuation in the *valor castral* will be about 50% of the market value. The example above is effectively for a property with a market value of 200,000€.

In the case of residents there is no deduction, but residents who own more than one property will be subject to tax on their second home. In this case the *renta* is added as income for income tax purposes. In the example above 1,100€ is added as income as if it were more earnings. This means they pay tax on this at their normal income tax rate. At the lowest tax rate of 15% the bill is 165€ which can be split in two if the second property is jointly owned.

WEALTH TAX

Impuesto extraordinario sobre el patrimonio is referred to simply as *patrimonio*. It applies to both residents and non-residents but wealth tax affects each group differently. A resident is required to declare their worldwide assets while a non-resident declares only their property and assets in Spain.

Wealth is calculated by totalling all assets and deducting all liabilities. Assets include property, car, boat, a business, value of Spanish bank balances, life insurance, jewellery, stocks, shares and bonds. The value of property is the highest of purchase price, fiscal value or value assessed by the authorities. Deductions are made for mortgages, debts, the vested rights in pension plans and any wealth tax paid in another country.

Residents are entitled to a general allowance of 108,000€ per person for all assets, plus an additional allowance of 150,000€ per person for a main residence making a total wealth tax allowance of 258,000€ per person. If the property is held in joint names each person is entitled to claim the exemption. There is no allowance for non-residents, who must pay wealth tax on all their assets in Spain, which for most people will consist only of their home.

After the allowance has been deducted (or not in the case of non-residents) wealth, defined as assets less liabilities per person, is taxed at a sliding scale beginning at 0.2%. A non-resident owner with a property of market value 200,000€ will pay 436€, or 218€ each for joint owners. A resident with a single property valued at 200,000€ will pay no tax.

Wealth up to €	Tax rate %	Cumulative tax €
167,000	0.2	338
334,000	0.3	839
716,000	0.5	2,751
1,337,000	0.9	8,335

Property tax

Many people view *renta* tax and wealth tax as one item, calling it *renta* and *patrimonio*, or even calling them a property tax. In the case of a non-resident, taking the example of a property with a market value of 200,000€, *renta* tax is 275€ and *patrimonio* tax is 436€, i.e. a total of 701€ per year for having a property in Spain (plus of course *IBI* and any community charges).

CAPITAL GAINS TAX

Liability for capital gains tax applies to residents and non-residents. Capital gains tax is payable on a profit from the sale of assets such as property, stocks and shares, antiques, art and jewellery. Since most ex-pats will have arranged their investments free of tax and non-residents will only have a property, capital gains in practice should only apply to the sale of a property. A capital gain is based on the difference between the purchase price and the selling price of a property, as stated in the *escritura*, less the cost of buying and selling.

Exemptions

- Residents aged over 65 are exempt from the profit made from the sale of their principal home, irrespective of how long they have owned it.

- Residents aged below 65 are exempt from CGT on their principal home, provided they've lived there for at least three years and plan to buy another home in Spain within three years of the sale.

- For both residents and non-residents, a property purchased before 31 December 1986 is free of CGT.

- Persons over 65 who contract to sell their principal residence in exchange for a lifetime right to inhabit the dwelling, along with a monthly payment – an equity release scheme – are free from CGT.

Tax rates

Non-residents are taxed at a flat rate of 35%. Buyers from non-resident property sellers are required to withhold 5% of the total purchase price and pay it directly to the tax authorities, making sure a seller is in part covered for CGT. Capital gains made by residents are treated as income and taxed in the year in which the gain was made, at a maximum tax rate of 15%.

Taxable gain calculation

1 Take the original purchase price entered in the *escritura* and add all official expenses incurred in purchasing the property which we know will be about 10% of the purchase price.

2 Increase the value above by the official inflation rate occurring between the time of sale and time of purchase. The Spanish government maintains official inflation statistics. So if the time between sale and purchase was six years and the official inflation in the same period was 12% then the value above is increased by the inflation factor of 1.12.

3 Take the selling price in the *escritura* and reduce it for any selling expenses such as estate agents' commissions.

4 Subtract 2 from 3 above to establish the capital gain which is taxed accordingly.

Additional reduction for buyers between 1987 and 1994

Property owners in this category have the right to an additional 11% reduction per year. So if a property was bought in 1990 the tax liability above is reduced by a further 44%.

Examples

Let us take a non-resident purchasing a property in 1997 for 100,000€ and selling it six years later for 200,000€. Inflation is 12%, purchasing on costs 10% and estate agents' commission 10% on selling.

Purchase price	100,000€
Add cost of purchase	10,000€
Sub-total	**110,000€**
Add inflation @ 12%	14,500€
(A) Sub-total	**124,500€**
Selling price	200,000€
Less costs of selling	20,000€
(B) Sub-total	**180,000€**
Capital gain	**B – A = 55,500€**
Tax @35%	**19,500€**

A resident will have the gain added to earnings for income tax. Taxed at a lower rate of 15% the total liability is 8,300€.

13

Wills and Inheritance Tax

There is no exemption between a husband and wife where each holds joint ownership of a property. In many countries a property can be held in joint names. If one person dies the property passes automatically to the other person. This is not the case in Spain where each person holds an equal share. Upon the death of one person, the other is subject to inheritance tax when inheriting the other half.

MAKING A WILL

Which country?

A person with British nationality at birth will find that Spanish authorities permit an estate to be bequeathed to whomever they choose, so long as this is allowed by their own national law. However a Spanish estate is subject to Spanish inheritance tax. Anyone with assets in Spain should make a Spanish will disposing of their Spanish assets in order to avoid time-consuming and expensive legal problems for heirs. A separate will should be made for disposing of assets located in the UK. Make sure a UK will states clearly that it disposes only of assets in that country and make sure a Spanish will disposes only of assets in Spain.

Spanish inheritance law applies theoretically to British citizens with a property in Spain. Both Spain and the UK have laws which state the disposal of property will be governed by the law of the country in which the property is located. However, a Spanish Certificate of Law ensures that when a foreign property owner dies, the disposal of any assets in Spain will be governed by the deceased's own national law, not Spanish law. Confusing and contradictory!

In practice the Spanish authorities do not ask if a testator is an official resident or not. They accept as valid a Spanish will disposing of Spanish property according to the law of another country. The only requirement by Spanish authorities is payment to Spain of inheritance tax on property or assets located in Spain.

UK laws

UK law (England, Wales and Northern Ireland) permits free disposal of an estate. Scottish law requires that some portion of the estate be left to surviving children. In other words an estate in whole or part can be left to anyone including the dogs' home. Compare this to the restrictive laws of Spain which are known as the law of compulsory heirs (*herederos forzasos*).

Spanish laws

Spanish inheritance laws restrict the testator's freedom to leave their property to anyone. Spanish law requires a testator to divide the estate into three equal parts. One third must be left to the children in equal parts. Another third must also be left to the children, but the testator may decide how to divide it with the surviving spouse having a life interest in this part. A life interest is a controlling interest as the child who inherits it cannot dispose of it freely until their surviving parent dies. The final third of the estate can be willed to anyone.

This is not quite as brutal for the surviving spouse as it may seem initially, as he or she keeps all assets acquired before the marriage, half of the assets acquired during marriage, and all inheritances which have come directly to the spouse. In effect this means that half of the assets do not really form part of the deceased person's estate. Half the property continues to belong to the surviving spouse.

Example

So what is a possible outcome of all this? Take a married Spanish couple with two children. One of the parents dies and they own a property which if sold is worth 150,000€.

The spouse retains 75,000€ acquired during marriage. The value of the estate is the other half which is obviously 75,000€.

Each child is allocated half of one third of 75,000€, in this case 12.500€ each.

Let us say the eldest son retains one third, in this case 25,000€, with a controlling interest, called an *usofructo*, held by the spouse.

Probably the final third of 25,000€ is left to the spouse. The spouse's total holding is now effectively 100,000€ with a controlling interest in a further 25,000€; in total 83%.

Spanish inheritance laws are inflexible. They aim to preserve the family unit by ensuring a property is handed down from generation to generation. In this example the property now has three owners and all three have to agree before it can be sold. An extremely unlikely scenario! More likely would be one child buying out the other child's share upon the death of the other parent.

Contesting a Spanish will

The laws of both the UK and Spain state that the inheritance laws of the country will apply where the property or asset is situated, but Spain chooses not to apply this provided inheritance tax is paid to them. So what happens when a British citizen leaves a Spanish property to a dog's home, which is perfectly possible under English law, but children contest the will, stating they are entitled to two thirds of the asset under Spanish law? After all, the Spanish authorities are choosing not to apply their own laws. Answer – the children would not win the case. It is better to eliminate grounds for contesting a will if a controversial one is to be written.

Dying intestate

If a UK resident or non-resident dies intestate, the estate in Spain will be distributed according to Spanish laws. If a British resident or non-resident dies with only an all embracing will for all assets this will still be applied, but there will be some considerable delay and cost occurring before it can be finalised. Specialist legal assistance is necessary in both countries. This is a strong argument for making a Spanish will.

How to make a will for Spanish assets

Making a Spanish will for Spanish assets according to the inheritance laws of the UK is quite straightforward provided the *abagodo* and *notario* understand they are not rubber stamping Spanish succession laws. A husband and wife who each own half a property as stated in an *escritura* are required to make separate wills as they own their share separately. A will is made out by an *abagodo*, authorised by the *notario* and signed in the latter's presence by witnesses. It is called a *testamento abierto*, the notary keeping the original with the testor receiving an authorised copy. Notification is made to a central registry in Madrid, called the *Registro Central de Ultima Voluntad*. Wills are filed there under a reference number and name of the notary.

INHERITANCE TAX

Domicile

There are many issues that can affect liability for inheritance tax, including the country of domicile.

Under UK law it is necessary to have a country of domicile for tax purposes. This will usually be the place where a person has the closest connection – normally a country of birth rather than a country of residence.

If not intending to return to live in Britain, it may be possible to establish an alternative domicile by taking steps to show a new home abroad is permanent. A person would then be classed as UK non-domiciled which can be extremely advantageous for tax purposes in an obscure tax haven, but definitely not Spain.

So to put it simply, a UK citizen, with a UK passport, resident or non-resident in Spain, is still domiciled in the UK unless steps are taken to change this. Although this assumption is made for the balance of this chapter it is to some extent irrelevant, for inheritance tax for Spanish assets is paid to Spain.

Guidelines

Inheritance tax is regarded by many as the cruellest of taxes. Having spent a lifetime paying income tax yet another lump of assets amassed over the years will be claimed back by the tax authorities. With careful planning people need pay little or nothing in inheritance tax. It was once described as a voluntary levy paid by those who distrust their heirs more than they dislike the *Hacienda*.

On death, the surviving spouse or dependants have six months to inform the authorities and pay any inheritance tax. If this is not done, with the property remaining in the deceased's name, it cannot be sold. There are also penalties for the non-payment of Spanish inheritance tax on time.

Spanish inheritance tax is payable when an inheritor is a resident of Spain, or the asset inherited is property in Spain. Spanish inheritance tax is not payable if the asset is outside Spain and the recipient is not a resident in Spain.

Inheritance tax is the liability of each beneficiary and not of the deceased's estate. Surprisingly the actual tax payable is based on four factors:

- the amount bequeathed
- tax exemptions and allowances
- the relationship of the recipient to the deceased
- wealth of the recipient.

There is no exemption between a husband and wife where each holds joint ownership of a property. In many countries a property can be held in joint names. If one person dies the property passes automatically to the other person. This is not the case in Spain where each person holds an equal share. Upon the death of one person, the other is subject to inheritance tax when inheriting the other half.

Spanish inheritance taxation law does not recognise a common law spouse. The relationship has no legal standing. They have no inheritance tax exemptions. They are also taxed at a premium rate, being treated as non-relatives.

Inheritance tax structure mirrors the Spanish law of 'compulsory heirs' and takes an old-fashioned view of marriage.

Setting a value for the deceased's estate

Property is valued either at market value, a value in the *IBI* statement, the value in the *escritura* or a value set by the *Hacienda*, whichever is greater. Stocks and shares, cars and bank accounts are valued at the date of death. The value of life insurance settlement is dependent on the recipient. Furniture, clothing and personal effects (*ajuar*) are treated as gifts having no value.

Exemptions

The law provides an individual exemption from tax of the first 16,000€ bequeathed where an estate is passed to a spouse, parents, children, brothers and sisters. This exemption applies to each inheritor, not to the total estate. For uncles, cousins and nephews, the exemption is cut by half to 8,000€. For more distant relatives, people not related and common law couples, there is no exemption. Conversely children aged 13 to 21 years of age attract higher exemptions. This applies to residents and non-residents.

Inheritance tax can be significantly reduced where a resident of Spain leaves a principal residence to a spouse, children, a brother or sister (over 65 years), who has lived with the deceased for two years. All are eligible for a 95% exemption in inherited value up to a maximum of 120,000€. To qualify, the *residencia* must have been held for three years, the property must have been lived in for three years and the inheritors must undertake not to sell the property for ten years. This exemption is only for a home or a family business and does not apply to investments or second homes. Non-resident holiday home owners cannot take advantage of this exemption.

The tax table on the next page is a rounded abbreviated extract from a full table. It is for guidance only. To use this table take the amount inherited, less any allowances highlighted in the previous section, subtract any debts owed by the deceased such as an unpaid mortgage and funeral expenses. This is the taxable amount with corresponding tax payable.

Inheritance tax tables		
Taxable amount	Tax payable	Tax
8,000€	600€	7.5%
16,000€	1,300€	8.0%
32,000€	2,900€	9.0%
48,000€	4,700€	9.8%
64,000€	6,800€	10.6%
80,000€	9,200€	11.5%
120,000€	15,600€	13.0%
160,000€	23,000€	14.4%
240,000€	40,000€	16.7%
400,000€	80,000€	20.0%

Table 1. Extract from inheritance tax tables: basic tax rates.

Wealth of inheritor €	Multiplying coefficient		
	A	B	C
0 to 400,000	1.00	1.60	2.00
400,000 to 2,000,000	1.05	1.70	2.10
2,000,000 to 4,000,000	1.10	1.75	2.20
+ 4,000,000	1.20	1.90	2.40
A = children, adopted children, grandchildren, spouses, parents, grandparents			
B = cousins, nieces, nephews, distant relatives, descendants and ascendants			
C = all others, including unmarried partners			

Table 2. Inheritance tax multiplier.

Tax Table 2 multiplies tax payable in Table 1 by a factor ranging from 1 to

2.4 depending on the wealth of the recipient and their relationship to the deceased. In fact Table 1 only applies to children, adopted grandchildren, grandchildren, spouses, parents and grandchildren who have a personal wealth less than 400,000€. All other benefactors, including those with high personal wealth and unmarried couples, pay more.

The Spanish inheritance tax system penalises inheritance to non-relations and to the rich. It is designed to maintain a family structure and benefit the poor.

Regional variations

Madrid, Catalonia and Valencia have different inheritance tax rates. Madrid has inheritance laws stating that unmarried couples can take advantage of the lower tax rates applied to married couples providing they are on the local register of unmarried couples.

Andalusia tax authorities have eliminated inheritance tax for individual family inheritors who are official residents of Andalusia and receive less than 125,000€. The 95% allowance also rises to 99.9%. The total value of the estate should not exceed 500,000€ and the wealth of each inheritor should not exceed 400,000€. Registered unmarried and same-sex couples also obtain this exemption.

These regional variations now recognise and come to terms with some of the old fashioned principals of Spanish inheritance tax.

Examples

In order to better understand the computation of inheritance tax, three examples are chosen. They all start with a property valued at 300,000€

held in joint ownership. One person dies and bequeaths the other half of the property to the surviving spouse. They have two children. The examples look at different combinations of resident, non-resident, married and non-married. For the benefit of simplicity the figures are rounded and the location is not one with regional tax variations.

1. Married couple, non-resident – a typical holiday home owner

Value bequeathed	150,000€
Allowance	16,000€ (individual exemption)
Taxable amount	134,000€
Tax payable	18,000€

2. Married couple, resident – a typical ex-pat

Value bequeathed	150,000€
Allowance	136,000€ (120,000€ + 16,000€)
Taxable amount	14,000€
Tax payable	1,300€

3. Unmarried couple, resident

Value bequeathed	150,000€
Allowance	nil
Taxable amount	300,000€ (multiplying coefficient of 2.0)
Tax payable	55,000€

In the first example the total inheritance tax bill would be halved if the property was left in equal parts to the children and surviving spouse. In the third example the tax bill would be 1,300€ if the couple married or lived in Andalusia.

LEGITIMATE METHODS OF AVOIDING SPANISH INHERITANCE TAX

Over the years many methods have been used to lessen the impact of this tax. Some of these have been illegal, and lead to greater problems and higher taxation at a later date. These methods have included the non-declaration of death, under-declaring the value of assets and using a power of attorney after death. With the introduction of new European tax laws on disclosure these practices will become a thing of the past. No professional advisor will risk high fiscal penalties for the sake of assisting clients in evading taxation.

Trusts

One such method is to create a trust, in which assets pass into the hands of a company, with each family member becoming a share holder. When one member dies, the shares are transferred to other family members. This attracts little tax. The location of this company may be offshore. Making a trust is best left to experts. It attracts annual charges and therefore is best suited to large financial holdings. The only real alternative to a will is to set up a trust structure during a lifetime. With careful planning this can eradicate delays, administration costs and taxes, as well as giving other benefits. For these reasons the use of trusts can be quite dramatic. A trust is not dissimilar to a will except that assets are transferred to trustees during a lifetime, rather than assets being transferred to executors on death. The trust deed is comparable to the will.

Usufructo (life interest)

You can transfer the property to a chosen heir while still alive and maintain a *usufructo* over it, retaining a right of use while living. The ownership has formally passed to another person. This legal move, which is viewed by the tax authorities as a gift, still attracts some inheritance tax, albeit at a reduced level, depending on the age of the people involved.

A simpler solution can be achieved by selling the property to a chosen heir. We do know that selling a property will cost around 10% of its value so in the previous examples this will be 30,000€. Compare this to the tax bill for an unmarried couple! A life expectancy of five years is however necessary as tax authorities assume – quite correctly – that this is to avoid tax.

Equity release

Some companies are offering an equity release facility to individuals owning a property in Spain. However, this should not be confused with schemes offered in the United Kingdom and certain other countries where elderly individuals accept a lump sum payment in lieu of the sale of their property, and continue to live in it rent free for the remainder of their lives. After their deaths the beneficiaries have no financial interest in the property as legal title belongs to the lender. This form of arrangement does not exist in Spain.

Most of the equity release schemes in Spain are in effect re-mortgages.

These schemes allow a property owner to take out a mortgage, normally without capital repayments, against the security of his or her property. Provided the borrowed funds are properly reinvested outside of Spain, this is likely to reduce Spanish inheritance tax on death. The loan can be as much as 100% of the property valuation for suitable applicants, and most lenders will agree the loan in most leading currencies, although the interest rate will vary according to the currency chosen. The lender may allow some of the loan monies to be utilised as so wished, but will require most of it to be invested and offered as further security for the loan. A typical loan is for a five-year period, after which it would have to be renegotiated. The lender may not be obliged to renew and may demand repayment at the end of the original loan period.

To avoid inheritance tax in this way all the normal rules must be followed. For a Spanish tax resident, the mortgage will reduce net assets in Spain. Of course, the loan proceeds must be invested outside Spain, either via a trust for beneficiaries or in a will to non-Spanish residents. If not a Spanish tax resident, the mortgage proceeds must be invested outside Spain and should not pass to any Spanish residents on death.

These equity release schemes only aim to reduce Spanish inheritance tax; if domiciled in the UK at death these schemes will not reduce any UK inheritance tax liability.

Give it away

This is by far the most generous concession on inheritance. It allows anyone to give away anything they like, including cash, property or works of art, with no tax liability whatsoever. Again there is one condition – the gifting person must remain alive for at least five years after making the transfer.

Investments and UK inheritance tax

Think carefully about where investments are located. It may be that investments are better located in an offshore trust, so this requires no further consideration as they should be protected by some tax avoidance scheme. Investments can be located in the UK or in Spain, in which case they should be allocated to the will of that particular country. It is just a matter of doing some calculations. UK inheritance tax liability does not accrue for the items listed below, after that the tax rate is 40%.

* Anything given to a spouse.

* Any gift to a charitable body.

* The value of an estate less than £275,000 (excluding anything given to a spouse).

* Anything given more than seven years before death.

* Gifts made before death if they did not, in total, exceed £3,000 in any one tax year.

Equalising a UK estate not exceeding £275,000 in value means it is exempt from UK inheritance tax, so married couples should try to equalise their estates to take full advantage of this exemption. If a husband whose wife is wealthy in her own right leaves his entire estate to her, he would only be adding to the potential charge on her estate upon death. Instead, he should consider leaving all or part of his estate directly to other beneficiaries – his children, for example.

Maintaining a loan

Inheritance tax is only payable after debts have been deducted. If it was possible to have a 100% interest only mortgage or loan then this is a guarantee of no inheritance tax. This is not possible as a mortgage but is possible as a loan. It is a matter of doing the figures. Some financial advisors are only too pleased to do it! Charges are high.

Holiday home owners

A Spanish holiday home owner will probably have a main residence in the UK which will be subject to the inheritance laws of that country. In fact the deceased's worldwide assets will be subject to the laws of the UK even if inheritance tax has already been deducted in Spain for the Spanish property. In this situation any tax paid in Spain can be deducted against a UK tax liability to avoid a double tax charge.

14

Learning About Culture and Customs

Ten Euros for a menu del dia, *or for three* tapas *and some wine, is excellent value for money. Glass in hand, soaking up the warmth of the sun and watching the world go by, puts one very close to the seven heavens of the cosmos depicted at the Alhambra, Granada.*

A SLOWER PACE OF LIFE?

Why do we say the Germans are boring, the Italians hot-headed, Swiss secretive, French awkward and the Dutch rather nice? This is a description of people but not the culture of a nation, which can be defined as civilisation, customs, lifestyle and society.

A Spanish guide taking a coach tour of Germans, Scandinavians, Swiss and some British to Gibraltar described it as 'typically English'. When pressed he said the pubs, the fish and chips shops were a way of life in England. That's how others see the Brits! This may not be liked, but that's how it is. Incidentally Gibraltar, in addition to pubs and fish and chip shops, is full of tax free electrical and liquor outlets. The tourist attractions play patriotic songs such as *Land of Hope and Glory*.

Spaniards have a zest for living and commonly put as much energy into enjoying their lives as they do into their work. Time is flexible, many people organise their work to fit the demands of their social life, rather than let themselves be ruled by work or the clock. All big cities have a buzz and all rural areas have their tractors and carts, but two undisputed facts support the view that a slower pace of life prevails in Spain. One is the intense midday summer heat which makes even small movement impossible. The other is *manana*, a deeply rooted Spanish attitude which frustrates the British and does permanent damage to German relationships. It causes difficulties, but in truth it is a way of life that says time is not important, tomorrow will do.

FAMILY GROUP

The family group is strong with sometimes two or three generations living within one house. The Spanish love of children is well known. Children will be beautifully dressed with a confidence that befits offspring in the new millennium. Mother and father will be proud parents with a deep sense of honour. Grandparents will be friendly, courteous, generous, not fully comprehending the staggering changes which have taken place since their childhood.

The young macho male will study in the evening for personal advancement, watch football and own a fast scooter. The beautiful dark haired senorita will be slim, wear flared trousers, and somehow be one foot taller and one foot narrower than her mother. Traditionally the man expects his wife to be the provider of love and affection and keep a clean home worthy of her husband. But this is changing fast, with Spanish women seeking more freedom and equality alongside their more worldly sisters.

At the weekend the family group will come together along with an assortment of aunts and uncles. With military precision, in a long line, they will make their way to the edge of the sea, each carrying an essential item for the day's outing. Parents will be first, loaded down with food, grandparents next with deck chairs, uncles with umbrellas, aunts and children with buckets, spades and balls. They will have a great time with a babble of excited conversation, interspersed with a shout, a wave of the hand, a shake of the shoulder, or a kiss in greeting or farewell.

TRADITIONAL SPAIN

Fiestas celebrate a national religious occasion or a local thanksgiving where towns and cities come to a stop as men, women and children dress up to enjoy themselves aided by a plentiful supply of food, wine and laughter. Processions with music start the evening, dancing and singing follow. Fireworks close the evening with a loud colourful bang. Each fiesta has its own distinctive character – sounds, colours, flavours, smells, costumes, rituals and a typical dish. There are celebrations for the dead and the living. Some fiestas appease the forces of nature. Others drive out evil spirits. Often they are based on historical events or include medieval or ancient customs. There is always a fiesta somewhere. They can last for a day, a week or a fortnight.

Perhaps the best known fiesta is the one celebrating the reconquest of the Moors by the Christians, held at Alcoy near Alicante but also replicated in many other Spanish towns in that region. Throughout the world there are many colourful processions but few can compare with the medieval pageantry which is accompanied by the music of brass instruments and loud kettle drums, as the marchers slowly sway rhythmically in the early darkness of a summer's evening.

Flamenco has its home in Andalusia, being traditionally performed by gypsies. It is more than just a dance, it is an expression of life, improvising to the rhythm of the guitar. Just as important, however, is the beat created by hand clapping and by the dancers' feet in high-heeled shoes. Castanets, solo singing and graceful hand movements are used to express feelings of pain, sorrow or happiness. Flamenco is best seen in Sevilla, modified for mass audiences and tourists, but still a fiery, individualistic performance.

In the southern cities of Cordoba, Granada and Sevilla a bullfighting poster is a common sight. Indeed, in some shops it is possible to have your own name printed on one. This is where the glamour ends. Hemingway understood bullfighting but modern Europeans do not, seeing it as a cruel, bloody sport, shocking and not for the faint-hearted. The Spanish see it as an art, a colourful spectacle where the skill of the bullfighter is pitched against the raw aggression of the bull. 'Six brave bulls' the poster reads, but the bull does not win, sometimes dying, at teatime, on live national television.

Bull running, made famous in Pamplona but also practiced in many

Spanish towns, offers the bull better odds. In this case the young macho male is the one in danger. The bulls are let loose in the streets of a town. Aspiring men run to avoid their horns. A few are injured and some die.

Despite the rich heritage of traditional Spain, football and even more football has now taken over as a main leisure pursuit. Sunday night is for watching football on large screen television in bars and restaurants.

Religion

Catholicism is still an influence in Spanish society. Although church attendance is falling, on a Sunday around midday families can be seen dressed in their best attire strolling home from their place of worship. The images of saints watch over shops, bars and drivers' cabs. Traditional fiestas mark church feasts.

EATING OUT

Food is important. Spaniards enjoy café life. Like the French they live to eat, not eat to live.

Breakfast is a coffee with bread or a croissant. There are three popular types of coffee. *Cafe solo* is a small cup of strong coffee, not for the thirsty. *Cafe con leche* is coffee with milk. *Cafe americano* is a large cup without milk. *Churros* – a doughnut type fried pastry with hot chocolate – forms a traditional breakfast of mega calories.

Lunch takes place between 2 pm and 4 pm and outside the home will consist of *tapas* or alternatively a light three-course meal with wine and bread. The choices for the *menu del dia* are chalked up on a blackboard outside the restaurant. The starter (*primero*) is soup, salad or pasta, the main course (*segundo*) is meat or fish and the sweet (*postre*) is fruit, ice cream or flan. It is a good example of simple food, at a fixed price, to be enjoyed with some wine. This meal would be served at a café, bar or restaurant. It would be eaten by workmen, office staff, tourists and residents alike.

Dinner is late – 8 pm to 10 pm. It is usually a repeat of lunch, but with a bit more wine and a bit less food. No one wants to go to bed on a full stomach.

The *tapas* bar is unique to Spain. Rows of dishes are arranged in a chilled cabinet in front of the customer. A choice is made, with bread and coffee or wine, to be eaten at the counter, at an adjacent table or at a table on the pavement or street. The offerings are made by the proprietor or by a local food preparation unit. They comprise tortilla, spicy meat balls, big plump olives, sausages, fried aubergines, egg salad, courgettes, spicy potatoes, liver, cheese, serrano ham, sardines, prawns in garlic, anchovies, mussels, fried squid, *calamares*, *sepia* (cuttlefish) and small fish in olive oil.

Ten Euros for a *menu del dia,* or for three *tapas* and some wine, is excellent value for money. Glass in hand, soaking up the warmth of the sun and watching the world go by, puts one very close to the seven heavens of the cosmos depicted at the Alhambra, Granada.

LOOKING, TALKING AND TAKING PRIDE

Outside the restaurant, in the main square or along the promenade the evening *paseo* commences with young girls and boys, parents and grandparents strolling in a leisurely manner. For some it is gentle exercise in the cool of the evening, for others a prelude to a good night out, for spectators it is an entertainment. In villages chairs are placed in its narrow streets, oblivious to passing traffic, as occupants emerge from their houses to talk and gossip about the day's events.

One important characteristic to be relied upon is Spaniards' readiness to communicate. Compare the discreet silence of a group of English people who do not know each other to the friendly chatter which quickly develops among a group of Spanish people. A good deal of social life is maintained *en la calle* (in the street) or any public place. Bars are particularly important. Spaniards generally enjoy conversation, invariably loud, where everyone seems to talk at once in an excited babble of noise.

Streets are clean and free of litter. Housewives sweep the street outside their home. Houses when occupied are kept well painted on the outside and owners fill their balconies and window boxes with brightly coloured flowers. Towns have ample and elegant street lighting and an almost total absence of graffiti! This is civic pride.

THREE POLICE FORCES

- *Policia Municipal* are the local police who dress in blue. They operate independently in a town and have a separate section for traffic control.

- *Guardia Civil* (National Guard) police rural areas. Their uniform is olive green. They deal with traffic and traffic offences.

- *Policia Nacional* (National Police) wear a blue uniform and operate in towns with a population greater than 30,000. They are concerned with crime.

All three police forces carry truncheons. The *Guardia Civil* and *Policia Nacional* carry guns. They are tolerant and polite except when dealing with major crime.

SHOPPING EXPERIENCE

The Spanish shopping experience is quite different with specialist family-run outlets forming the bulk of sales activity. This is however changing fast, with out of town shopping centres springing up everywhere, but in the cool of the evening, with a stop for a *café con leche* or a *tapas*, indulging in a multilingual conversation with the occupants at the next table, shopping can still be a pleasurable activity.

Tiendas

The smaller *tiendas* (shops) are cheerful, friendly, helpful places where the owners and assistants are anxious to please. This is also where the annoying Spanish characteristic of 'not forming queues' is seen at its worst. People push and shove to the front to be served. This is best dealt with by patience as the perpetrators of this behaviour are often elderly who seem to think that their advanced years entitle them to non-queuing privileges. Alternatively say *perdone* and address the sales assistant, who usually knows what is happening.

Opening hours for *tiendas* vary between summer and winter, but normally are 9.30 am to 1.30 pm and 4.30 pm to 7.30 pm Monday to Friday, plus a Saturday morning. The afternoon siesta seems inappropriate in winter but essential in summer, when the shops open later, as no one wishes to go shopping during the intense heat. There is, however, pressure from businesses and other Europeans to change this custom. Banks and some organisations open at 8 am and close at 2.30 pm. Holiday resorts, restaurants and hypermarkets which open seven days a week, 12 hours a day, have already squeezed the siesta out of existence.

The *tienda* retailing backbone is highly specialised.

- bread shop   *la panaderia*

- butcher   *la carniceria*

- cake shop   *la pasteleria*

- chemist   *la farmacia*

- clothes shop   *la tienda de ropa*

- delicatessen   *la charcuteria*

- fruit shop   *la fruteria*

- fishmonger   *la pescaderia*

- grocer   *la tienda de comestibles*

- hairdresser   *la peluqueria*

- ironmonger   *la ferreteria*

- launderette   *la vanderia*

- newspaper stand   *el quiosco*

- shoe shop   *la zapateria*

- travel agent   *agency de viajes*

- tobacconist   *el tabac.*

Hypermarkets

French-owned hypermarkets such as *Carrefour* and *Intermarché* dominate food retailing. Smaller German supermarkets such as *Lidl* and *Aldi* compete on price but not on product range. Spanish companies such as *Mercadona* are now gaining a firm foothold. Hypermarket shopping is an experience not to be missed, with everything possible being sold under one roof: clothes, footwear, garden plants and equipment, sports goods, bicycles, electrical goods, hi-fi, furniture, DIY, motoring accessories, kitchenware, toys and books. The food hall has a massive product range. The fruit and vegetables are highly colourful. The delicatessen counter is staggering in its variety of sausage and cheese.

The fish counter is laden down with salmon, trout, mussels, skate, mackerel and a whole range of unrecognisable species. The wine, spirits, soft drinks and bottled water section stretches for miles. These hypermarkets have 40 to 60 checkouts. Staff are equipped with roller skates to get from point to point. Franchised within the same building are restaurants, banks, jewellers, newsagents and the National Lottery.

Clothing

There is one major, famous, clothing chain store in Spain – *El Corte Ingles*. It has a similar marketing strategy to other European retailers, selling mainly male and female clothing together with books, CDs, electrical goods, computers, kitchenware and sports equipment. Price points are similar to or higher than the rest of Europe with only occasional sales (*rebajas*).

With the exception of a large number of international sports brands, clothing is not yet fashionable outside big cities. It is conservative in taste, for Spain is not yet a fashion centre, its citizens sticking to fairly traditional styles.

European chain stores, like European banks, have only a few outlets in major cities. The marketplace may be penetrated by individual foreign brands but not by foreign retailers. Where they do exist they tend to be a poor relation of their national parents.

Out of town shopping

It is here where change is happening. Electrical chains, computer stores, sports clothing and equipment shops, fast food chains, cinema complexes … the lot, are being built everywhere. They are not like British style shopping malls but based more on the outdoor USA experience.

Open air markets

There is a profusion of mobile open-air markets, often stopping normal activity in a town for one day each week. People flock from kilometres around to buy hams, fish, fresh fruit and vegetables. Clothing too is sold, together with some ceramics and leather goods. Beware of purchasing designer items, watches and jewellery as they may be fakes.

Bargaining takes place, but it is an unnatural custom for northern Europeans. Want to bargain? Express an interest in an item. Haggle on price. Say 'no' and walk away. The stall owner comes after you. That's when you get the low price, not before.

The hustle and bustle can be of some interest, but be cautious. Pickpockets, operating in gangs of two or three, are often present at open-air markets.

Mercado central

A central market is run by the local council. Most towns have one. They are efficient, clean, hygienic purveyors of fish, meat, pastries, fruit and vegetables, a traditional alternative to supermarket shopping. Little English is spoken but a smile accompanies each purchase.

- Anything else?   *Algo mas?*
- That's all   *Eso es todo*
- Thank you   *Gracias*

Strangely, Spanish fresh fruit and vegetables have to be purchased with care. Locally grown produce in season is cheap and available all year long, but of course like all European countries Spain exports most of its Class I produce. Quality produce is better purchased from the *fruteria* at the *mercado central* than from a supermarket.

Tabac

One other national institution has to be mentioned – the *tabac*, a state owned tobacco shop selling all brands of cigarettes, cigars and tobacco at very low prices: 20 Euros for 200 cigarettes is quite normal. It is fairly obvious from these prices that many people still smoke. In bars and restaurants, shops and public places, the cigarette is still part of the Spanish way of life. The *tabac* has other functions. It also provides government forms for taxation and sells postage stamps. Never stand in a long queue at the main post office for stamps when a *tabac* is nearby.

Wine and olive oil

Best buys in Spain, apart from tobacco, colourful ceramics and leather products, are undoubtedly wine and olive oil, both agricultural products from tightly regulated industries.

The Mediterranean countries of Italy, France and Spain all produce good quality wine under various climatic conditions. Spain produces excellent wines but their product marketing has been poor, leaving France holding the premium market and Spain operating at the bottom end. Tighter government regulations have seen a continuous rise in wine quality but not in their marketing strategy.

There are about 55 officially designated wine-producing areas, all individually indicated by a small map on the label on the back of each bottle. Each area has a number of measurable standards specified for the product.

There are broadly three main wine-producing areas: the north, of which *Rioja* is by far the best known; the central area best known for *La Mancha* wines, and the southern area, which produces aperitif wines and sherry. *Rioja* is a strong red wine comparable to any French product but considerably cheaper. In the best tradition of wine regions its annual vintage is classified as poor, normal, good, very good or excellent.

No one makes a fuss about drinking wine. At an equivalent cost to a soft drink or a bottle of water, it is the natural accompaniment to a meal. Branded wine, with an individual number on the back of the bottle, blended house wines, *vino de mesa* (table wines), young wines or supermarket brands at two to three Euros per bottle are all exceptional value for money.

There are 400 million olive trees in Spain with 80% growing in Andalusia. Driving around Cordoba and Granada you can see fields and fields, acres and acres of olive trees set on the undulating landscape. The experts in Brussels say there are too many; olive oil production is too high. *Aceite de Oliva* (olive oil) is used in cooking, in salad dressing and as a substitute for butter and margarine. Some people say it is olive oil, together with fresh fruit, vegetables, and fish which makes the Spanish diet so healthy.

DEALING WITH THE POST

Correos, the national postal service of Spain, is easily identified by the yellow signs outside each post office. Yellow is also the colour of mail vans, delivery scooters and mail boxes. Mail to and from Europe is automatically sent air mail. Delivery of mail in Spain can be slow. The post office offers a range of services. Registered or express mail, parcel post, redirection, private boxes and banking are all available.

Spanish post offices can be small and dark with long, slow moving queues. Go to the *tabac* for stamps. One price covers all EU countries:

• Ten stamps for Europe, please. *Diez sellos para Europa, por favor.*

Letters are delivered to a household door or American-style to a driveway gate. On urbanisations all the post boxes are grouped together beside a focal point such as a swimming pool. It is necessary to go to the post office to collect parcels or registered mail where identification may be required.

Competition exists for the Spanish postal system. Mail Boxes Etc., an American company, has a number of offices in Spain. Although still dependent on the services of *Correos* it operates independently for overnight international parcel delivery through companies such as UPS and FedEx. It also offers a mail box service, shipping and packing, fax printing and photocopying. It sells office supplies and stamps. This enlightened company is refreshing to deal with but its activities are restricted by protectionism offered to the state postal system.

Getting names and addresses correct

Spanish names are important. A mother's maiden name is added to the end of a full name. Women do not change their name when they marry. The formal prefix of *Don* or *Dona* is introduced at the start of a name.

Senor Don John Frederick Smith King is simply Mr John Smith with a middle name Frederick and a mother's maiden name King. He is married to Senora Dona Maria Dolores Sanchez Vicario. Got it? Who is Conchita Smith Sanchez? Yes, correct, their daughter Conchita. Telephone books can be fun!

An accurate address is also important:

Sr Smith
Calle Madrid 27, 2
03189 Orihuela Costa
Alicante

Translated this means:

Name	Mr Smith
Number/Street/Floor	27 Madrid St. 2nd Floor
Post code town	03189 Orihuela Costa
Province	Alicante

The zip code 03189 is made up of 03 as the province number and 189, the post office number.

COMMUNICATIONS

Television

This medium is now dominated by digital TV. Most ex-pats want to tune into English language programmes. These can be found on Sky digital systems via a satellite dish. To enjoy the marvels of this technology you need to have a set top box installed together with the appropriate multi-sized satellite receiving dish to have access to hundreds of channels of television and radio. Television companies who supply the smart cards, such as Sky, cannot legally send cards direct to an address abroad since they have copyright only for a UK audience. However, a number of satellite dish installation companies in Spain can supply cards.

Urbanisations may offer a better selection of English, French, German, Scandinavian and Spanish channels through an underground cable system.

There are several Spanish television stations but Spanish television is dominated by pay-as-you-view programming of films and football, together with standard news, documentaries, music, soaps and old films.

Radio

A mention should be made of radio. Spanish FM stations are available by the dozen, all featuring music and endless chatter. More interesting, however, are the popular UK based FM stations available by satellite. These stations are received by digital receiver or by a separate FM cable. To complement all this activity are a number of new 24-hour English language FM stations giving a unique blend of local news, chat and music.

Telephoning

Telefonica (the Spanish telephone company) charges for calls, line rental and telephone rental. The tariffs are for local, national and international calls. Time tariffs exist for peak, normal and night time. Peak times are 8 am to 8 pm Monday to Friday, and 8 am to 2 pm on Saturday. Emergency telephone numbers are published in the white pages of the telephone directory and also in English language weekly newspapers.

Telefonica has competition for its landline service from cheap call operators but, like many major companies, it meets this competition head on with price reductions and special offers. *MoviStar* is the mobile phone company of *Telefonica* which has far greater competition from *Vodafone* and other companies.

Computers

Of course it is possible to buy a new computer in Spain, although there are not as many large computer superstores as there are in Britain. A computer bought in Spain will probably come loaded with Spanish software and there are also slight changes to the Spanish keyboard as the keys have to deal with a language which has accents over some letters.

One accessory worth installing for your computer and television equipment is a surge protector. Spain does experience frequent surges in the electricity power supply and this can damage sensitive equipment.

Newspapers

Local, national and international; daily, weekly and monthly; Spanish and English; expensive, cheap and free publications, all clog the news-stands. Spanish daily newspapers are mainly middle class. *El Pais* (*The Country*) and *El Mundo* (*The World*) have lots of pages aimed at the serious reader and are cracking good value for money. At the bottom end of the Spanish daily press content is devoted solely to football.

All the European daily newspapers are available. They are printed in Spain but cost three times more than the national edition. Weekend newspapers also have some sections missing. The best reads for the ex-pat are the locally printed English language weekly newspapers. They are a good blend of national and local news, lots of gossip, information and adverts. Indeed some of the small ads are reminiscent of standing inside a central London telephone box!

Popular English language books are more difficult to find but large and small English bookshops do exist. Specialist titles are best purchased through e-commerce.

15

Enjoying a New Lifestyle

... a bewildering choice of activities only handicapped by an ageing process, which probably rules out bullfighting, bungee jumping and hang gliding. Football, rugby, running and hockey are now passive, watching sports as a battle with the waistline is probably lost too.

GET OUT AND ABOUT

Owning a property in a new country calls for a change in outlook. It is a transition from one culture to another. For some it may be a shock. It is important to accept a different lifestyle. Adapt, embrace the challenge and enjoy life.

About 12 million people whose native tongue is English, will visit or reside in Spain in any year. The European Commission, in a survey, states that only 3% speak Spanish. A lack of command of a second language puts them at a severe disadvantage when communicating and integrating into the Spanish way of life.

The influx of foreign residents is not evenly spread throughout Spain. Some towns have developed as foreign enclaves. New urbanisations are marketed heavily in one country but not evenly across all countries, giving rise to colonies of people who rarely understand the culture of Spain.

Of course there is the sun worshiping and the *cerveza* drinking but the novelty of that soon wears off since it can only lead to boredom or alcoholism. This will hopefully be replaced with a more positive attitude to life: getting out, learning about the country, developing new interests and meeting new people.

LEARN ABOUT THE COUNTRY

The real way to learn about a country is to travel. There are other methods, such as reading books and tourist guides, which are colourful and informative. Watching travel films too has its place, but it is only by going to see a place that true its ambience can be experienced. There are places where you can enjoy the sun, the sea and the mountains. There are places where you can benefit from the climate and keep in shape with your favourite all year round sport, where you can discover local history and monuments, travel down hidden byways and forest tracks, participate in local fiestas, meet local people … and much more.

Jump into a car and go! On minor country roads the traffic is amazingly light, even in the height of the holiday season. Go 20 kilometres inland and there is virtually no traffic on roads throughout the year. Getting around is a pleasure but avoid *autopistas* and *autovias* for at rush hour they can be no better than the M25.

ENJOY SPORTING ACTIVITIES

The diverse geographical nature of Spain, with its mountains, woodlands, beaches and sea, gives a wonderful backdrop for sporting activities. Golf clubs, sports centres, bowling greens, gymnasiums, swimming pools, marinas and tennis clubs are all striving to make better use of leisure time. The newcomer faces a bewildering choice of activities only handicapped by an ageing process, which probably rules out bullfighting, bungee jumping and hang gliding. Football, rugby, running and hockey are now passive, watching sports, as a battle with the waistline is probably lost too. A short cycle ride to the supermarket seems to be more appropriate than dressing up each Sunday in matching bright lycra outfits, ripping calf muscles to shreds, ascending narrow mountain roads astride the latest 21-gear machine.

No! It is time to put the more active stuff on the back burner. Slow down. Remember, this is Spain – where time is not important. Consider the less athletic pursuits where skill, knowledge and abilities can be honed to perfection with practice, practice and more practice. Golf and bowls perhaps! Tennis or maybe hiking! Tone up at a gym. Take up fishing.

Golf

A hundred years ago the screaming, jumping and beating of clubs on the ground was called witchcraft. Today it is called golf. Golf in Spain is booming, driven by tourism and the climate. The worldwide success of Ballesteros, Olazabal, Jimenez and Garcia has contributed to this success. Ballesteros is a star in Spain, an icon in Britain and if he had been Italian would by now have been painted on the ceiling of the Sistine Chapel.

The Costa del Sol is often referred to as Costa del Golf; such is the profusion of new courses. They are carved out of barren landscapes, pampered and watered to produce lush green fairways. Consequently golf is not cheap: 60€ for a round is common! In Scotland, the home of golf, it is a game for the working man. In Spain it is a game for tourists and wealthy residents.

Hiking

Walking or hiking clubs exist in all the main areas. For the adventurous, the best places to go are the Picos de Europe in Northern Spain, the Pyrenees near the French border, the Costa Blanca inland from Benidorm and around the Sierra Nevada near Granada. Strangely, hiking is not too popular with Spaniards but is hugely popular with new foreign residents.

Many holiday companies offer Spanish walking tours. This has given rise to some excellent English language publications describing good detailed routes with clear concise maps. Trails are way-marked and the only hazards encountered are dogs and the unhygienic nature of some refuge huts. It is important not to underestimate some of these rugged trails with snow on high ground, rapidly changing weather and steep paths.

Bowling

The capital cost to establish a bowling green is low. Demand is high. It is one of the few competitive sports for those of advancing years, which combines well with social activities. Such is its popularity on the Costa Blanca that a winter league of nine clubs has a full page devoted to its activities in the local weekly paper.

Sailing

Adapting to the demands of a thriving tourist industry has led to the growth of pleasure craft harbours of which there are now hundreds stretched along the Mediterranean coastline. They range from small harbours that cater for a fishing fleet and dinghies to large, glitzy harbors such as Puerto Banus close to Marbella, which can cope with 1,000 boats, many being no more than a display of wealth or floating gin palaces. It is hardly surprising that marinas are full to capacity but they do offer a full selection of services at a reasonable price, and of course the Customs authorities allow foreign registered boats to be used for six months of the year and to remain in the country for the rest of the year during which time the boat maybe used for habitation.

The development of marinas and new harbours has spin-offs such as ships' chandlers, shops, restaurants, bars and up-market apartments. Yachting is for the rich and it is dinghy sailing for the rest of us. The Med can be choppy. Unfortunately there are not too many totally sheltered bays and regrettably even fewer supervised dinghy sailing clubs.

Fishing

So popular is fishing that the basic equipment is sold in supermarkets or newspaper shops. Sea fishing from the shore is still a sport for the youngster with only the smaller species being caught. River or lake fishing in Northern Spain is a far more serious matter altogether, with trout and salmon, pike and carp available. The local tourist office is the place to enquire about licences, season tickets and such like.

Tennis

Tennis is practiced everywhere. It has been made popular by the many Spanish superstars. It is a low capital cost, highly popular activity. Every small town, hotel and club has its tennis courts utilised all year around. Many urbanisations, in addition to having a swimming pool, have a tennis court maintained through the community charge.

Running

It is not too hot to run! Spain, like all countries, has its runners and joggers. It has superstars too. It has often been host to international athletics meetings. Each town has its own sports ground complete with a running track. Marathons and half marathons are commonplace – but not in summer.

Gyms

Many privately run gymnasiums tend to be devoted to muscle building. But northern Europeans much prefer the weight reduction clubs of bright lycra, cardio-vascular training, running and cycling machines, sauna and steam bath. Modern gymnasiums exist, located in new building complexes.

Baring all on the beach

While France accepted nudism, it was not until the early 70s that topless sunbathing appeared in Spain, even though the patrolling *Guardia Civil* advised people to cover up. Today it has changed with the practice common and nudism allowed in certain designated areas.

The first nudist resort appeared in 1979 near Estepona on the Costa del Sol but other beaches, about 60 officially designated and other unofficial ones, are widely accepted as locations for naturism.

Irrespective of what is worn, Spain now boasts the highest number of Blue Flag beaches and marinas in Europe. The Blue Flags are awarded where the cleanliness of the sea water is up to standard and environmental management, education, safety and the provision of services have been approved. Keep updated on **www.blueflag.org**.

Skiing

Ever heard of the Costa Blanca Ski Club? It sounds unreal. The Costa Blanca is sun, sea and sand! Literally hundreds of skiers travel from the Costa Blanca and all parts of Spain to the Sierra Nevada each year. It has several unique features as it is the southernmost ski centre in mainland Europe and is also one of the highest, giving a long season with good sunshine, lasting until May. It is only 150 kilometres from the Costa del Sol and 400 kilometres from the Costa Blanca.

Just outside Granada the resort is well developed with hotels, parking for thousands of cars and buses, 20 ski lifts capable of carrying 30,000 people per hour, 54 kilometres of marked slopes and 3.5 kilometres floodlit for night-time skiing at weekends. Equipment hire and lessons present no problems – only doing it causes difficulties.

The area is well named. It is called *Solynieve* (sun and snow).

Sports federations

There are many other sports available – squash, skiing, beach and water sports, horse riding, mountaineering, gliding, cycling, and of course football, football and more football. Each sport has its own federation, which is always a good starting point for information.

MIXING SOCIALLY

Foreigners seek their own wherever they go, but perhaps the English-speaking do so with more enthusiasm than other nationalities. Some pursue intensely social lives within the community while some deliberately shun the company of their compatriots. In the early stages of visiting Spain the support received from other expatriates is often important in cementing friendships and forming social networks. The newcomer is typically ascribed a subordinate or dependent role, seniority among expatriates being mainly determined by their length of residence. A second influence is the degree of permanence versus seasonality of residence, as long-term residents tend to look down on tourists, even those of their own nationality.

In 1992 the BBC filmed an ill-fated soap drama near Mijas, creating an image that the British expatriate community on the Costa del Sol lived in an artificial world. The programme was based on a conceived stereotype of 'Brits in Spain' presenting them as living an idle existence in the sun, drinking too much alcohol, behaving like old colonials, and certainly not integrating into the Spanish way of life. Sometimes the ex-pats were portrayed as having a wonderful time, on other occasions as being poor and isolated, while the presence of a few exiled criminals was turned into all manner of stories.

Of course it is not true! While British residents rarely integrate effectively with local Spaniards, they enjoy a well-structured lifestyle which on the whole keeps them busy, happy and healthy. They also join the many expatriate clubs, which cater for a wide range of activities and interests. Many people join these clubs to meet people of similar background and interests and to widen social circles. Social clubs are a method of meeting people, of sharing a common interest, past or present. They are meeting places to deal with problems or to seek information and are an aid to settling in a new country. Golf and hiking may be the top sports but a meal, a drink or a visit to a club are the main social activities.

RELAXING

A siesta is a wonderful Spanish institution traditionally intended to protect people from the heat of the midday sun. It has been carried forward to today. There is something wonderful, particularly in the summer months, about drawing the curtains and lying down for a couple of hours in the afternoon. Many quickly learn to appreciate a siesta, even stray cats and dogs.

Spain's *manana* attitude can help people to relax and become more philosophical. Does it really matter if there is a delay so long as emergencies are dealt with as they happen? Does it matter if there are queues, it does not seem to bother the locals and what's the point of getting upset?

Driving a few miles inland, the buzz of the coast disappears. Park the car and just walk in the countryside and you are immediately struck by how calm everything is. Of course you hear the sounds of nature, birds singing, strange rustlings in the long grass made by some unseen creatures, noise of the breeze in the trees overhead, but at other times there is almost complete silence. Go higher into the mountains, stop for a few minutes and just listen to … nothing.

Ordinary everyday chores can become a source of pleasure and wonder. The simple action of rising late or early, every morning to blue skies, looking towards a green golf course, mountains or sea and thinking 'am I lucky or not?'. At the end of the day when skies are clear and a brilliant canopy of stars covers the heavens, the same thought occurs.

16

Avoiding Failure

In Southern Spain the phenomenon of Sahara rain occurs once or twice per year. Rain clouds moving north from the Sahara desert deposit a thick, red dust on new, clean, white houses.

A NEED TO LEARN

This book is about success. Success in realising a goal. Success in achieving a dream. For some people, no matter how hard they try, life in Spain is not for them. Whatever the reason they return home saddened by the experience. We need to learn from these situations.

A property bought on a whim, the difficulty of visualising a home from a plan or drawing, high pressure selling, financial problems or difficulty in absorbing Spanish culture may be reasons for rejecting a life in a new country. Fortunately these reasons for failure are few and far between, for if there is a will to do so, these problems can be overcome.

A true explanation for people going back home probably lies elsewhere.

CASE STUDY

Employment

It had been an excellent night out. Local singers had put on fantastic, popular entertainment of a high professional standard. We followed it up with a good meal and some wine. At around 2 am last drinks were taken in a Spanish bar.

An English couple, in their late 30s or early 40s, were sitting on their own. They looked forlorn. We asked them to join us for 'one more'. It transpired this was their last weekend in Spain. They had sold their property and were returning home.

They were curious to know why we liked Spain so much. We too were curious to know what had gone wrong with their attempts to build a new life. Apparently they had come to Spain to work and live but after three years had not been able to obtain suitable employment. Neither could speak Spanish.

We listened sympathetically. Not a lot could be done at this late stage. No point in giving advice when a decision had been made and implemented. Yet the solution was blindingly obvious. Learn Spanish!

If a good vocation is required in Spain it is absolutely essential that you speak the language. If not, the only employment available is working in an English-speaking bar or restaurant or setting up your own business servicing English speaking clients.

ON THE DOWNSIDE

Holiday homes

The purchase of a holiday home is financially sound when property inflation is taken into account. Inflation however is not cash flow and the annual outlay for flights, running costs and taxes all mount up, and may be more than a budget allows. A permanent holiday home is also great, but using it to a maximum constrains holidaying elsewhere.

Female residents

Female permanent residents find it harder to settle in Spain than their men folk. Family and grandchildren can be missed. While this wrench can be minimised by holidays, the psychological barrier of time and distance is still an obstacle.

Sahara rain

In Southern Spain the phenomenon of Sahara rain occurs once or twice per year. Rain clouds moving north from the Sahara desert deposit a thick, red dust on new, clean, white houses. This disconcerting act of nature necessitates a major clean up with brushes, water and power hoses.

Retirement

At the end of a long working life retirement is a goal richly deserved, but it can be hard to stand back and relax. The cut and thrust of business can be missed, particularly when entrepreneurial opportunities in Spain are clearly obvious.

People may have been married to each other for 40 years, but living in each other's company for 24 hours per day, seven days per week is a new experience. Tensions can develop.

Nothing to do

Boredom can be a killer. After the house is sorted, the car running smoothly and the garden done, what happens next? It is important to keep an active mind and body, for the soporific heat of the Spanish sun will soon slow senses. Sun worshipping, a daily gin and tonic or serious *cerveza* (beer) drinking can make for an easy life, but only in the short term.

A free holiday

A move to the sun and suddenly it is amazing how many 'friends' are acquired. Of course it is wonderful to have visitors, but if you are not careful it is very easy to end up running a hotel and taxi service. It is necessary to differentiate between close friends, those who want to come and stay, and the others who see it as a free holiday.

Style of construction – noise

The style of construction of a new property can be a negative: the problem is noise from neighbours. Methods of construction used in apartment blocks, townhouses and duplexes can lead to easy transmission of sound through the building. A typical apartment block depends for its strength on a framework of concrete pillars and floors and the walls are simply added to this framework. Since the framework is common to every apartment the noise generated by work underway in another apartment, not necessarily immediately next door, can be transmitted through the entire structure. Marble floors are wonderfully cool in summer but can also cause noise transmission problems.

Over-development

Spain has the climate, the laid-back lifestyle and also a booming property market whereby the whole of the Mediterranean coastline between France and Gibraltar is almost covered in concrete; so developers are now moving inland. The Mediterranean coast is now for the development of hotels, apartment blocks and townhouses. Very few villas are under construction since a piece of land that could support one villa could probably support an apartment block instead. Villas built along the coast several years ago are now having their line of sight affected by over-development.

Builders show no consideration to people who live close to their building sites. Builders drive heavy trucks over existing pavements and drains and in the process damage them. They drive lorries full of earth through residential areas, scattering mud or dust over existing roads.

Tolerance

A more complex reason exists for people returning home. It has nothing to do with bricks and mortar, nothing to do with the physical aspects of change, nothing to do with Spain. It is about human relationships. Back home, people have spent 40 or so years achieving their position in a class-divided society, represented on one level by their place of residence. The detached house in Oslo, the apartment in Dublin, the block in Frankfurt, the cottage in Antwerp, the terraced row in Burnley are all forgotten and replaced by a single-status society of what you are now and not what you were. Since equality on the urbanisation is the name of the game, it is hardly surprising tensions occur.

Primary groups form: the golf fanatics, the night owls, the heavy drinkers, the restaurant dwellers, or simply those who wish to gossip. Others may want to keep to themselves. Either way they may get on with each other, or they may not. Tolerance is needed: tolerance to accept different lifestyles, different needs and different backgrounds.

But tolerance is rarely given because the need for it is seldom understood.

AND FINALLY ...

It would be wrong to end this book on a negative when Spain has so many things to do and so many places to see. There is the cordiality of the people, the incomparable scenery, the beaches of fine sand, the days of sunshine, the high mountains, the vast plains, the nightlife, the evenings, the magnificent cuisine, the restaurants …

Too many hours or too many pages are necessary to say what Spain has to offer. There is only one way to be sure; come and see it for yourself. Spain for a holiday home, for work, for a long-term stay, or for retirement can be a step into the unknown. But if some simple preparation is undertaken it can be a step into sunshine and happiness.

Let the dream be fulfilled!

Appendix 1

A PURCHASE CONTRACT ISSUED BY A BUILDER FOR A NEW PROPERTY

Place .... Date ....

Parties

On the one part is the Vendor .... registered with number .... living at .... represented with power of attorney by .... with *NIE* number ....

On the other part, as Purchaser(s) .... with UK Nationality and .... with UK Nationality living at .... with passports numbers respectively of .... and ....

Both parties consider each other to have sufficient legal power to enter into this purchase and sale contract by mutual agreement.

Statements
One:

.... is the sole owner of a plot of land situated inside the *Plan Parcial* .... with number .... in the municipal district of

.... It was acquired by virtue of private contract signed with .... The plot is free of loans and charges. The deeds of the planned urbanisation have been registered at the Registry Office of .... It was signed on .... before the Notary ....

Two:

On the above mentioned area will be built 458 bungalows as per plans and drawings prepared by Master Architect .... living at .... The builder is .... living at .... who reserves the right to modify the number of bungalows or apartments or the project itself, if necessary, due to architectural or town planning reasons.

Any modification of the project for technical or legal reasons will be agreed by the town hall or the architect, or the master builder.

Three:

That among the bungalows or apartments is number .... in the urbanisation of .... with a usable surface of approximately 64 square metres, a built one of 76 square metres and a plot size of approximately 100 square metres consisting of the following elements:

A duplex with three bedrooms, dining-sitting room, kitchen, bathroom, toilet, terrace and solarium.

Four:

The Vendor .... is interested in selling the described property and the Purchaser .... in buying it, according to the following clauses:

Clauses

FIRST .... sells to ....
who buys the property described in the third statement of this contract.

The selling is carried out with all rights, facilities and services which
are inherent in the sold property, the results of the building project and
the development rules including the proportionate part, corresponding
to the communal element zones of the urbanisation.

In the sale are included all the communal rights of the urbanisation
called .... The maintenance of the communal
area is paid by the owners for the present and future phases.

SECOND The total agreed purchase price of the property amounts to
.... Euros plus the corresponding Value Added
Tax (*IVA*). This sum will be paid as follows:

• **When the purchaser signs the contract they will pay the amount**
  of .... Euros in cash.

• **On .... the purchaser will pay the amount of**
  .... Euros with a cheque made out to
  ....

• **On .... the purchaser will pay the amount of**
  .... Euros with a cheque made out to
  ....

• **The balance of the total price will be paid by the purchaser**
  when they sign the *escritura* plus 7% *IVA*.

THIRD .... will deliver the property described
in the third Statement of this contract in the Month of
.... approximately.

FOURTH The date of delivery of the property will be notified to the Purchaser by the Vendor the moment the property is finished and in a correct condition to be used and at this date the Purchaser will take charge of all communal expenses of the urbanisation and any other costs which may be derived from the maintenance of the communal aspects of the urbanisation.

FIFTH In the event the Purchaser is not able to pay the amount of one or more of the payments on the established date, which is indicated in the second clause of the contract, and notifies the Vendor in writing, the Purchaser can pay the balance with corresponding interest.

As compensation for non-fulfilment of the Contract, the Vendor will keep 50% of each paid sum that the Purchaser should have made to the date on which the Vendor decides to resolve the contract.

SIXTH Upon the agreed price being paid in full, plus cost of the applicable taxes and other agreed obligations, the Vendor will grant to the Purchaser the *Escritura* to be issued before the Notary nominated by the former, in the city of .... within a period of 15 days from the date of payment.

SEVENTH The Purchaser undertakes to respect and follow the obligations established in the statutes of the urbanisation to which the described property belongs, authorising the Vendor to constitute the Community of Owners, which will follow the Initial Statutes and approve new Statutes together with all the co-owners according to the Horizontal Property Law. Likewise the Purchaser authorises the Vendor to contract water and electricity on their behalf. Until the Community of Owners is formed the Vendor is authorised to take the necessary measures for the correct administration of the community.

EIGHTH All extra expenses derived from the purchase of the property (water and electricity connection, Notary and Registry, documented juridical acts, etc.) will be paid by the Purchaser, who authorises the Vendor to the draw up water and electricity contracts. After the date of delivery of the property the Purchaser will take care of all the water and electricity expenses occurred by the property. If on completion the electrical company *Iberdrola* has not made the connection for the electrical meters, the Purchaser promises to send to the Vendor receipts for consumption. When completed the Purchaser will pay a deposit of .... Euros representing costs for the next few months. When the meters are fitted the Vendor will adjust the payments. If the Purchaser has paid too much the Vendor will return the balance and on the contrary if the Purchaser has paid too little, they will pay the difference to the Vendor.

NINTH *IVA* (Value Added Tax) will be set according to Spanish legislation.

TENTH For any legal matter between the Vendor and Purchaser as notified at the heading of this contract, where the Purchaser is a non-resident, it will be submitted to their legal address.

ELEVENTH The property is exclusively allowed to be used as a dwelling house.

TWELFTH In the event of any dispute arising from this contract, the parties submit themselves expressly to the Courts and Tribunals of .... and their superiors, or by default the Courts and Tribunals of .... renouncing any others to which they might otherwise be entitled, as this document shall be governed according to the Laws in Spain.

THIRTEENTH The Vendor guarantees the strict fulfilment of everything stated in this Contract and is not obliged to do anything which is not written in the Contract.

FOURTEENTH Furniture, curtains, lamps, covers, mirrors, electric units or any ornamental units are not included in the sale price of the property.

FIFTEENTH It is obligatory for all foreigners in Spain to have a fiscal number (*NIE*) (Spanish Legislation, Decree of 2nd February 1996, Article 61).

Both contracting parties hereof being in conformity and agreement with the above, sign this Purchase Contract in duplicate in the place and on the date first before written.

The Vendor .... **(signature)**

The Purchaser .... **(signature)**

APPENDIX 2

COMMUNITY RULES

The aim of the following STATUTES is to stipulate the rules owners must observe in order to ensure smooth functioning of the Urbanisation and maintenance of good relationships between neighbours.

All those deeds which have not been included in the STATUTES OF THE COMMUNITY OWNERS are to be resolved according to the HORIZONTAL PROPERTY LAW 49/1960 AND POSTERIOR REFORM BY LAW 8/1.999, published on 8 April 1999.

The Property

1. The *escritura* describes the services and facilities of each property. According to Law 8/1.999, chapter 11, Art. 7, each property owner can modify the architectural elements, facilities or services of the property provided the security of the building, exterior appearance, general structure or shape is not changed or diminished, and the rights of other owners are not prejudiced.

2. The owners or occupants of the property are not allowed to carry out activities which are forbidden in these statutes, harm the building, or infringe general laws with bothersome, unhealthy, dangerous or illegal activities.

3. All owners are under the following obligations:

    a. When using the facilities of the Community and other communal elements, whether they are for general or private use, to make good and avoid any damage.

    b. To keep the house and garden tidy.

    c. The house is to be used exclusively for residential purposes.

    d. The grills, walls, awnings and all the external elements must follow a model approved by the Community.

    e. To contribute to the general expenses of the Community proportionate to the amount appearing in each *escritura*, the final date for payment being one month from date of invoice.

    f. To communicate to the Secretary-Administrator of the Community an address in Spain to receive receipt of notification and summons from the Community. In the absence of this communication, the address will be taken as the owner's property in the Urbanisation. The notifications handed to the occupants will take judicial effect.

    g. According to the previous paragraph, if it was impossible to issue a notification or summons addressed to an owner, it is understood that it will be placed on the Community notice board or on other visible place of general use, signed by the Secretary-Administrator and with the approval of the President. A notification made by this means will have the full judicial effect.

    h. To keep silent during the rest time, from 14.00 to 16.00 hours in the afternoon and after 24.00 hours.

i. Rubbish and gardening waste is to be deposited in the rubbish containers, by means of well-closed plastic bags.

j. Repairs and any other building works which have been authorised by the Community, do not imply the right to obstruct the pavements and/or road with building material, except for cases in which it be necessary. In these cases the materials are to be deposited in as little space as possible, keeping the area clear for pedestrians and vehicles. When the works are finished the owner is obliged to clean the area leaving the pavements and road in a perfect condition.

k. All domestic animals must be accompanied by their owners and leashed when out of doors. Furthermore, the owner will not allow domestic animals to relieve themselves in the Urbanisation, and if this happens the owner will pick up the excrement.

Community Board

4. The managerial posts of the Community are as the follows:

4.1 President

4.2 Vice-President

4.3 Secretary

4.4 Administrator

4.5 Board Members

All the managerial posts are elected for one year. All those designated can be removed from their post before the expiration of the period by agreement at an Extraordinary Meeting of Property Owners.

5. The President is to be designated from among the owners by
    election or draw. The designation is to be compulsory, although the
    owner designated can demand their relief to a Judge one month
    after their election, giving due reason. The Community will consult
    with a Judge when the Meeting could not appoint a President of the
    Community.

    The President is to hold full legal representation of the Community
    in all matters concerning the Community.

    The length of the appointment is one year. It is possible to re-elect
    the President at the Ordinary General Meeting by majority of those
    owners present. In this case, the President is allowed to refuse the
    post without the need to state a reason.

5.1 The President is to have a mobile telephone.

5.2 The General Meeting is to approve a cash turnover of 1,200 Euros/
    year. The President is to have available this amount for small
    repairs, works or improvements, without having to consult the
    General Meeting and justifying this expense by means of
    corresponding invoices.

5.3 All those works, repairs or improvements which exceed the amount
    allocated to the President to be agreed by the General Meeting,
    from at least three different estimates.

6. The Vice-President is to take responsibility for standing in for the
    President in their absence or inability, as well as to assist them in
    their work according to the terms established by General Meeting.

7. The duties of Secretary and Administrator are to be carried out by
    the President, unless the hiring of a Collegiate Administrator by

means of the present statutes is agreed (Chapter 11, Art. 13, Paragraph 5, Law 8/1.000).

Communal Areas

8. The floor, projections, foundations, party walls and other elements described in the article 396 of the Civil Code and Law 49/1.960 of 21 July are communal elements. So too are the inside streets of the Community, gardens, swimming pools, TV and FM installations, lighting, toilets and other facilities.

9. It is prohibited to make any modification, work or repair to the referred communal elements if it has not been approved by the General Meeting of the Community, who should request a technical feasibility report and the pertinent licences.

10. No owner can claim the right to a parking space in their garden, since in no title deed is it stated the garden should have access for vehicles or inside parking. If the property has vehicle entries in the garden it will depend on the goodwill of the neighbours to keep this access clear. Bulky vehicles, trucks, big vans and machinery cannot be parked in the private streets of the Urbanisation. The vehicles parked in private streets must be moved to the other side of the street every 15 days, in order to clean the streets. All those vehicles parked in the private streets for more than two months are to be removed to a nearby place. In this case the crane hired to remove the vehicle is to be paid by the owner.

11. All owners must observe the Statutes, informing the President of any infringement, in order to take any necessary measures according to the seriousness of the infringement or damage caused.

Use of Swimming Pools

12. The swimming pools, as communal areas, are at the disposal of all owners, who must respect them at all times.

13. According to the Decree 25511997 of 7 December, by the Valencia Government, which regulates the Hygienic-Sanitary and Security rules for swimming pools, Article 2: the area made up of the vessel or vessels and the surrounding area destined for swimming, as well as the installations and facilities necessary to ensure the perfect functioning and performance of the recreational activity, are to be defined as the swimming pool.

14. The two swimming pools belonging to the Urbanisation are catalogued as private swimming pools, since they do not have more than 200 m^2 of water lamina (surface).

15. The swimming timetable is to be from 10.00 to 21.00 hours, during the summer months, the entry controlled by means of swipe cards issued by the Administrator and with the approval of the President. For the remainder of the year only the second swimming pool is to be open.

16. Since both swimming pools are defined as private, it is not necessary to hire lifeguards and therefore the Community declines any responsibility for accidents inside the facilities, except in the case of those covered by the insurance policy taken out by the Community.

17. During the months of July and August two caretakers are to be hired, one for each swimming pool. The caretakers are to have the following tasks:

a. Working timetable: from 9.30 to 14.30 hours and from 16.30 to 21.00 hours.

b. To clean and remove rubbish from the swimming pool area, to disinfect the floor of the showers and if necessary to clean the bottom of the pool.

c. To check the performance of all facilities, recording any shortcomings, flaws or damages in a daybook.

d. To check the water condition at the beginning of the day and record the analytical parameters of pH and mg/1 of disinfectant.

e. To control the entry of users, by requesting the presentation of an updated card and denying admission to those owners and guests whose names appear on a blacklist provided by the Administrator.

f. To ensure the application of hygiene and security rules, avoiding personal confrontation at all times.

g. To facilitate access for disabled people and ensure that they have seating.

h. In case of an emergency or injury, the caretaker will call telephone number 112.

18. Children under 9 years are to be accompanied by their parents or guardians.

19. The use of flippers, playing with balls, and swimming without clothes, is not allowed.

20. It is also strictly forbidden to enter with animals, to bring bottles and glasses inside the swimming pool precinct, or to eat or drink, except snacks, in which case the tins, cartons and rubbish must be deposited in the rubbish bin.

21. Chairs, parasols, air mattresses and floats for adults are not allowed in the pool.

22. Solar creams must be eliminated before going into the water by means of a shower.

23. Everyone, without exception, must have a shower before going into the water.

Appendix 3

ESCRITURA

A deed of purchase and sale

Protocal Number ....

In .... (Name of town) my place of residence, on .... (Date).

Before me .... (Full name), Notario of this City and of the Illustrious College of Valencia.

APPEARS

Representing the party selling

.... (Full name), of age, married, inhabitant of this city, with address in .... (Full address) and with DNI number ....

And the party buying ....

Mr .... (name) of British nationality, of age, ... divorced, living in .... (Full address) and with Passport Number ....

He accredits his nationality with the document of identification before quoted but does not accredit his *NIE* and he is advised by me, the Notary, that according to R.D. of 2nd February 1996 in Article 61, it is obligatory for foreigners in Spain to have a Foreigners' Identity Number.

He confirms that he is Non-Resident and that the investment is not from offshore funds and is legal according to the RD 664/00 of April 23.

REPRESENTATION

.... (Full name) in representation with Power of Attorney for .... (Building company full name) formed for an indefinite time on the .... (Date) before the *Notario* of .... (Name of City) .... (Name of *Notario*) with the number of his Protocol .... with official *CIF*, number .... and office address ....

The object of the company is to promote, construct and sell for themselves or for others, all types of buildings with related operations, such as the purchase of land, urbanisation, parcelling, letting and administration.

THEY STATE

.... (Name of company) has complete and official power over the following housing urbanisation under construction.

Description

Within the boundaries of .... (Name of town), Plan .... the second phase of project .... a house with two floors joined by means of an

internal stairway. This one is marked commercially with the number
.... Looking at the facade from the east this is
the eighth of its type and there exists eight running from right to left.
There is independent access through the garden. There are surfaces
built, closed and indoors of 76 square metres and 64 usable square
metres, 12 metres distributed in terraces, various departments, rooms
and services. Looking at the front, at the right is the house with
commercial number .... and its garden, left the
street. Adjoining the bottom is a chalet with commercial number
.... and its garden.

Community Quota

The property is assigned a quota of the common elements, benefits and
charges in relation to a total value of 0.67%.

Inscription

The property is Inscribed in the Property Register of
.... (Town) book 1357, volume 1122, folio 13,
property 23456, first inscription.

Local Tax Contribution

Those appearing declare lack of the tax receipt because it is still to be
issued, which I have duly noted.

Title

Acquired for purchase by the commercial organisation
.... (Name of company purchasing the land)
stated in the deed granted on the .... (Date) before
the Notary of .... (Town)

.... (Name) number .... of his Protocol.

The new work and horizontal division is declared, before the Notary of .... (Town) .... (Name) the day .... (Date).

Origin

The house described forms part of the second phase of the group 'Al Andalus' comprising two phases; the first phase comprising 274 dwellings and the second phase 184 dwellings.

The second phase of the group urbanisation called 'Al Andalus', in the boundaries of Orihuela, in the urbanisation Partial Plan 'Las Piscinas' is composed of this residential group of 184 dwellings, of which 62 are ground floor, 62 are first floor denominated bungalows and 60 individual, denominated chalets.

It is built on the plot of land 73 (parcela EH.4.4), in the boundaries of Orihuela, belonging to the Part Plan 'Las Piscinas', Sector J-1, with a superficial extension of 19.668 metres square dedicated to high residential construction. North is the limit of the part plan, south the road, east Parcel EH.2.1, and west, parcel EH.2.3.

Charges

It is free of charges, except for any fiscal obligation of the tenants and lessees and the current payment of the quotas to the community declared by the sellers. The buyer accepts the Certificate sent by the Secretary, previously approved by the President.

The plot on which the properties are located is liable to the costs of urbanisation, in conformity with Article 178 of the Regulation of Administration of Urbanisations which has been endorsed by the sellers.

Information Registry

The notary makes known that the description of the property, its ownership and the charges, in the form previously referred to, are of the statements of the sellers, of the title of property shown to me and of the *Nota Simple* of the registration of the property, obtained by me, which I have seen.

Regarding the deed of new work and horizontal division mentioned in the title, which I have seen, I write the following:

Common Elements and the Law of Horizontal Property are the results of the application of Article 396 of the Civil Code and Law 49/1.960 of 21 July with the following:

1. The common elements are the floors, stairs, foundations, wall supports and party walls, facades, patios and other that determine Article 396 of the Civil Code and the services of combined use, not already referred to or included among the common elements.

2. The owners of the different elements finance their expenses and enjoy the rights of the common elements in the proportion marked by their corresponding quotas. Therefore the expenses of maintenance services, cleaning, surveillance, illumination etc that are used by all, will be distributed amongst all, using the previously established quota.

3. The administration of the common elements is commended to a Meeting of Owners, composed of a President, Secretary and others

that are named. Until such a meeting is constituted the administration will provisionally be conferred to a person or company named by the developer who undertakes the administration of this Urbanisation, even naming the corresponding administrators, being the honorarium of those in charge of other communities to fix the quotas to be paid by the owners conforming to the above number 2.

4. The apartments, no matter how many times the owners requests it, will not be the subject of regrouping, aggregation, segregation, division or subdivision, and in general any other modification, except for reasonable access as appropriate for opening new holes to common elements.

5. The area of recreation and swimming pool is designated inside the group green areas of size about 1,000 square metres. It will not be used only by the holders of the described dwellings, but also by the owners of the dwellings of the already declared phase 1 in the adjacent parcel that constitutes the group. Together with phase 1, this will finance the expenses of the use of the green areas, pool and recreation, in proportion to the useful surface of the dwellings.

6. The walls that separate the different elements of the group will be built following the pattern approved by the constructor with the object of uniformity within the urbanisation. No modifications or the use of ornamental materials can be undertaken without the constructor's previous consent.

7. The owners of the dwellings cannot cover the existing air vents located under the dwelling for ventilation.

8. The owners of the dwellings on the top floor, who enjoy the use of their terraces, are responsible for the cleaning of the existing drains,

it being their responsibility and not that of the constructor for smells and dampness.

9. The constructor reserves the right to put in the deed any modification, explanation, or rectification that is necessary for the good of the urbanisation provided such modifications do not alter the quotas of the elements already notified. The constructor reserves the right to alter the construction of certain elements in a different way to the one declared in this deed.

The commercial representative reserves the right to conduct, to constitute and to give rights, real or personal, to supply companies such as *Iberdrola*, *Aquagest*, *Telefonica*, or any other that is appropriate.

THEY GRANT

First The company .... as it is represented, sells the property described previously, free of obligations, as well as current taxes, with all its uses, rights and servitudes, to .... (Name) who buys it.

Second The agreed price is .... Euros (price in figures and words). The seller declares having already received part of the purchase price from the buyer who completes the transaction with a bank draft.

Third As is conventional to the contracting parties, all expenses to the making of this deed will be paid by the buyer including the Municipal Tax on the Increment of the Value of Lands.

Fourth The seller to receive from the buyer the Value Added Tax (*IVA*), that is to say 7% on the conventional price as entered in the Treasury publication.

Fifth The buyer agrees to accept the norms of the community and to have received a letter with a recommendation on maintenance from ………………………… (Name of the community administrator of properties).

Sixth The buyer recognises that, by virtue of this sale, they assume responsibility for the payment of light and water, and any other bills relevant to the house as well as carrying out any appropriate maintenance.

Seventh It is understood that the seller of the dwelling has given to the buyer a multi risk building insurance policy taken out with ………………………… for one year.

Eighth The buyer's names as their fiscal representative ………………………… (Name) ………………………… (Address).

They say this and they grant

I give them advice, legal and fiscal warnings, especially those with regard to the 30 working days for the authorisation of this deed, to liquidate the same, and to affect the Tax on Patrimonia Transmissions and Documented Juridical Acts, as well as being affected by the consequence of this Tax and the present document. I read this deed which is verbally translated into English for the convenience of the buyer, the translator being known by me, by name of ………………………… with residence in ………………………… and with residence card number ………………………… .

 I give again the warning made previously by me, the Notary, that the buyer had the right to an official translator but this was not required and finding that the document is satisfactory they sign, in the presence of the translator, with me the Notary, and that I publish the deed in nine legal pages of the series 3s, numbers 456789 to 8 numbers in sequence.

I GIVE FAITH

The signatures of those appearing are

.... (Representative of the seller with power of
attorney)

.... (Buyer)

.... (Notary)

.... (Translator)

Appendix 4

A PURCHASE CONTRACT DRAWN UP BY AN *ABOGADO*

Private contract of sale and purchase

At .... **(Address) on** ....
(Date)

GATHERED

On the one part,

The spouses Mr .... and Mrs
.... , of age .... , living at
.... (Address) with *DNI* numbers 44.55.66 y
23.24.25 respectively.

And the other,

Mr .... and Mrs .... of age
.... , living at .... (Address)
with current *residencia* numbers 56.57.58 and 43.45.46 respectively.

All present are in their own names and rights and are recognised to have the capacity to complete the private contract of sale and purchase.

THEY STATE

That the spouses Mr .... and Mrs
.... are the rightful owners of the following
property:

Urban dwelling, in a state of ruin, situated in ....
(Full address) comprising ground floor with room and coral, occupying
40 square metres.

Adjoining property: Looking from the street, right entrance belongs to
the heirs of Mr .... , the left entrance belong to
the heirs of Mr .... , the land at the back belongs
to the Hermitage of the Calvary, and in front of the dwelling is the
street.

It is inscribed in the Property Register of ....
(Town) in volume 1212, book 43, folio 12, house reference number
2.345.

CHARGES ON THE PROPERTY: MORTGAGE IN FAVOUR OF
.... **(BANK)** For 27,045 Euros for two years with
ordinary interest of 11.5%, and for three years delay interest of 17.5%
on 540 Euros for costs. Commenced 3.03.1996. Formalised in a Deed
on 13.03.1996 and authorised by the Notary of
.... (Town) .... (Name).

TITLE

The property belongs to the spouses Mr .... and
Mrs .... for the purchase made for the children Mr

.... and Mrs .... by virtue of
a purchase and sale *escritura* authorised by the Notary Mr
.... of .... (town) on
02.09.87 with reference number 745.

CLAUSES

FIRST That by virtue of the present contract the spouses Mr
.... and Mrs .... commit to
sell, and Mr .... and Mrs ....
commit to buy, the property previously described together with the
rights that are inherent. The property is sold free of charges,
encumbrances, mortgages or any other limitations that affect the rights.
The sellers commit to carry out whatever operations are necessary to
arrive at the date specified with a property in a completely free state
and stated correctly in the *escritura*.

SECOND The total price of the sale and purchase is
.... Euros.

A) Form of Payment: the buyers pay to the sellers a deposit of
.... Euros as part payment of the agreed total
sum.

B) The remaining sum of the total price of the sale and purchase
.... Euros will be paid by the buyers at the
moment of the signing of the corresponding *escritura*.

C) The signing of the corresponding public *escritura* will be before
.... (Date).

THIRD The expenses that are derived from completing the *escritura*
will be to the account of the buyer with the exception of the *plus valia*

which will be to the account of the seller. Also to the account of the seller will be all the charges derived from the cancellation of the mortgages as well as those for the work of amplification of the *escritura*.

FOURTH If the buyer, for reasons unaware to the seller, seeks to resolve the contract in an unilateral way, it is understood that the buyer will forfeit to the seller the amount already paid. In the case that the seller defaults double the amount will be returned to the buyer. Failure to pay the balance of the price .... Euros by the date .... will result in the resolution of this contract coming into effect.

FIFTH The contracting parties agree that any questions or problems that could be raised by reason of this contract are to be made expressly to the Tribunals of.......................

SIXTH Both parties designate the address given at the heading of this document in order to effect notifications, requirements, and citations.

The sellers and the buyers sign this present contract in duplicate in the place and date established in the heading.

Signature Sellers ....

Signature Buyers ....

Appendix 5

AN OPTION CONTRACT SIGNED ON BEHALF OF A CLIENT BY AN AGENT

.... and .... with Irish passports numbers .... and .... respectively, living at .... (Henceforth, the Buyers) are interested in purchasing the following property:

Number .... *Residencial* .... Urbanisation ....

This property is sold to them by the Agent .... with *CIF* number .... in representation of .... a UK citizen, resident in this property (henceforth, the Seller), and with the following *NIE* number.

....

Under the following stipulations:

First The agreed price is .... Euros. The purchase includes furniture, full kitchen appliances and items according to an attached list.

Second On signing this contract, the Buyers pay a reservation deposit of .... Euros to the Agent ....

the present contract serving as a receipt thereof. If the Buyers should breach any of the agreements established herein, they will lose the deposit. If the Seller should become in breach of this agreement, the Buyers are entitled to receive the deposit in double.

Third The Buyers accept to pay the remaining part of the total price .... Euros at the signing of the Title Deed, which will take place no later than ....

Fourth The Seller has the obligation to pay and cancel any debts, encumbrances, limitations or prohibitions that the property may have inscribed or not at the Land Registry.

Fifth All fees and taxes related to this agreement and to the Title Deed until its inscription at the Land Registry are included in the above price, except the *Plus Valia* tax which is the obligation of the Seller.

Sixth Any discrepancies that may arise between the parties with regard to the present agreement shall be resolved at the Law Courts of .... according to Spanish Law.

Signed in .... on ....

The Buyers ....

The Seller (Agent) ....

Appendix 6

COMMUNITIES OF SPAIN AND THEIR PROVINCES

The provinces of Spain are grouped into 17 autonomous Communities. Asturias is a *Principado*, Murcia is a *Region*, Navarra is a *Comunidad Foral* while all the rest are classified as *Comunidades*. Their full name, address, first two digits of the provincial postcode and the provincial letters used on older vehicle number plates are shown below.

Northern Spain

Comunidad Galicia, Palacio de Rojoy, 15705 Santiago de Compostela.

Galicia	15	A Coruna	C
	27	Lugo	LU
	32	Ourense	OR
	36	Pontevedra	PO

Principado de Asturias, Calle Suarez de la Riva, 33071 Oviedo

Asturias	33	Oviedo	O

Comunidad Cantabria, Calle Casimiro Sainz 4, 39003 Santander

Cantabria	39	Santander	S

Comunidad Pais Vasco, Palacio de Ajuna-Enea, 01007 Vitoria

Basque	01	Alava	VI
	20	Guipuzcoa	SS
	48	Vizcaya	BI

Comunidad Floral de Navarra, 31002 Pamplona

| Navarra | 31 | Navarra | NA |

Comunidad La Rioja, Calle General Vara del Rey 3, 26071, Logrono

| La Rioja | 26 | La Rioja | LO |

Eastern Spain

Comunidad Cataluna, Plaza de San Jaime, 08002 Barcelona

Catalonia	08	Barcelona	BA
	25	Lleida	L
	17	Girona	GE
	43	Tarragona	T

Comunidad Aragon, Diputacion de Aragon, Paseo Maria Agustin 36, 50071 Zaragoza.

Aragon	22	Huesca	HU
	44	Teruel	TE
	50	Zaragoza	Z

Comunidad Valencia, Palau de la Generalitat, 46003 Valencia.

Valencia	03	Alicante	A
	46	Valencia	V
	12	Castellon	CS

Region de Murcia, Palacio de San Esteban, Calle Acisco Diaz,
30071 Murcia

| Murcia | 30 | Murcia | MU |

Central Spain

Comunidad Madrid, Puerta del Sol 7, 28013 Madrid.

| Madrid | 28 | Madrid | M |

Comunidad Castilla La Mancha, Palacio de Fuensalida,
Plaza de Conde 2, 45002 Toledo

Castilla la Mancha	02	Albacete	AB
	13	Ciudad Real	CR
	16	Cuenca	CE
	19	Guadalajara	GU
	45	Toledo	TO

Comunidad Extremadura, Calle Jose Fernandez Lopez 18,
06800 Merida.

| Extremadura | 06 | Badajoz | BA |
| | 10 | Caceres | CC |

Comunidad Castilla y Leon, Plaza de Castilla y Leon, 47006 Valladolid

Castilla y Leon	05	Avila	AV
	09	Burgos	BU
	24	Leon	LE
	34	Palencia	P
	37	Salamanca	SA
	40	Segovia	SG
	42	Soria	SO
	47	Valladolid	VA
	49	Zamora	ZA

Southern Spain

Comunidad Andalusia, Palacio de San Telmo, Avda de Roma, 41071, Seville.

Andalusia	04	Almeria	AL
	11	Cadiz	CA
	14	Cordoba	CO
	18	Granada	GR
	21	Huelva	H
	23	Jaen	J
	29	Malaga	MA
	41	Sevilla	SE

Islands

Comunidad las Islas Balaeres, Calle Marina 3, Consulado del Mar, 07012 Palma de Mallorca

Balearic Islands	07	Baleares	PM

Comunidad las Islas Canarias, Plaza 25 de Julio 1, 35004 Las Palmas de Gran Canaria

Canary Islands	35	Las Palmas	GC
	37	Tenerife	TF

Appendix 7

PUBLIC HOLIDAYS

1 January	New Year's Day
6 January	King's Day
19 March	St Joseph's Day
March/April	Good Friday or Easter Sunday
1 May	Labour Day
25 July	St James' Day
15 August	Assumption of the Virgin
12 October	National Day
1 November	All Saints' Day
6 December	Constitution Day
8 December	Immaculate Conception
25 December	Christmas Day

The central government allows 14 days paid public holidays per year. Twelve national holiday days are highlighted above. Each region also celebrates its own holiday with additionally most towns and villages having their own carnival and fiesta days. If a holiday falls on a Tuesday or Thursday, shops and offices may be closed on the intervening Monday or Friday making it a long weekend.

Northern Europeans find the frequency of Spanish holidays confusing and ignore all but the main national holidays.

Appendix 8

ENGLISH LANGUAGE PUBLICATIONS

Costa Blanca News	Apartado 95, 03500 Benidorm. Tel. 966812841. www.costablanca-news.com
Costa del Sol News	Apartado 102, 29630 Benalmadena, Malaga. Tel. 952449250. costasol@dragonet.es
Lookout	Urb. Molino de Viento, Calle Rio Darro, Portal 1, 29650 Mijas. Tel. 952473090. lookout@jet.es
Spain	21 Royal Circus, Edinburgh. EH3 6TL. Tel. 01312267766. www.spainmagazine.com
Sur in English	Avda Doctor Maranon 48, 29009 Malaga. Tel. 952649600. www.surinenglish.com
The Broadsheet	Bear Publishing, Plaza de Canalejas 6, 28014 Madrid. Tel. 915237480.
Mallorca Daily Bulletin	San Filiu 25, Palma de Mallorca. Tel. 971719706. www.majorcadailybulletin.es
The Western Sun	38683 Los Gigantes, Tenerife. Tel. 922865998. www.thewesternsun.com

Appendix 9

COMMON QUESTIONS

What are the main advantages and disadvantages of moving to Spain?

Spain offers an excellent climate, low cost of living, good healthy food and drink and a relaxed lifestyle. Some disadvantages include a high petty crime rate on new urbanisations and lots of 'red tape'.

Is the culture different?

The excellent climate leads to many outdoor activities. Drinking plenty of wine and eating late at night is a Spanish custom. While fiestas, flamenco and bullfighting are the traditional romantic values of Spain, like many European countries café life and football dominate at weekend. There are many hypermarkets, but few departmental stores outside large cities. Small family run shops called *tiendas* and frequent outdoor markets make up the shopping experience.

What are we looking for in an estate agent?

Initially, someone who can offer a wide range of properties in the area of choice and secondly someone who will help in the difficult settling in process. A good agent will be a member of a professional organisation.

Do we need a solicitor and fiscal representative?

Most definitely yes to both. An *abogado* is someone who can complete
the legal process of buying a property and at the same time offer good
advice. A *gestor* is useful for dealing with routine administrative
matters and an *asesor fiscal* for dealing with taxation.

What additional costs are incurred when buying a new home?

It is wise to allow 10% of the purchase value to cover the costs of
conveyance and taxes.

How much does it cost to run a home?

About 3,300 Euros per year, covering electricity, water, telephone,
property insurance, taxes and community charges.

Tell me about medical facilities

In coastal areas, hospitals tend to be new. Private doctors, dentists and
medical centres are well advertised, staffed by highly qualified
Spaniards and some northern Europeans. Many drugs are available
without prescription from chemists who also offer advice on ailments.
Visitors from Europe can claim free treatment by the use of the EHIC
card. Residents below retirement age should take out a private health
insurance. Residents over retirement age, or disabled, are entitled to
free health care obtained through entering the Spanish health system.

Sporting facilities?

The countryside and sea provide a natural backdrop for all sporting
activities of which golf, bowling, tennis and walking are the most
popular for northern Europeans. For people not interested in sport,

social clubs exist for almost every type of interest.

Any myths?

Yes, one seems to constantly crop up. Upon death the Spanish government does not reclaim your property. Just do the normal thing; make out a Spanish will for Spanish assets.

Appendix 10

USEFUL PHRASES

Greetings

Hello	*Hola*
Good morning	*Buenos dias*
Good afternoon/evening	*Buenas tardes*
Good evening/night	*Buenas noches*
How are you?	*Que tal?*
Fine, how are you?	*Muy bien, y usted?*
See you later	*Hasta luego*
See you tomorrow	*Hasta manana*
Goodbye	*Adios*

Useful words

Sorry	*Perdon*
Please	*Por favor*
Thank you	*Gracias*

You're welcome	*De nada*
Of course	*Claro*
Yes	*Si*
No	*No*
Sir	*Senor*
Madam	*Senora*

Questions

Where's the station?	*Donde esta la estacion?*
Where is the hotel Melia Alicante?	*Donde esta el hotel Melia Alicante?*
How much is that?	*Cuanto es?*

Again

Pardon?	*Como?*
I do not understand	*No comprendo*
I do not know	*No se*
How do you write it?	*Como se escribe?*

People

| My name is ... | *Me llamo ...* |
| What's your name? | *Como se llama?* |

I'm Miss Pamela Smith	*Soy la senorita Pamela Smith*
Where are you from?	*De donde es usted?*
I'm from Ireland	*Soy de Irelanda*
What do you do?	*En que trabaja?*
I'm a nurse	*Soy enfermera*
I speak a little Spanish	*Hablo un poco Espanol*

Time

What time is it?	*Que hora es?*
It's one o'clock	*Es la una*
It's two/three/four o'clock	*Son las dos/tres/quatro*
It's half past three in the afternoon	*Son las tres y media de la tarde*
It's quarter to eleven at night	*Son las once menos cuarto de la noche*
What time do you open?	*A que hora abren?*
What time do you close?	*A que hora cierran?*

The home

bathroom	*el bano*
bed	*una cama*
bedroom	*el dormitorio*
chair	*una silla*

curtain	*cortina*
house in the country	*finca*
dining room	*el comedor*
flat	*el piso*
house with internal stairs	*duplex*
house	*la casa*
kitchen	*la cocina*
living room	*el salon*
old farmhouse	*cortijo*
room	*la habitacion*
sofa	*un sofa*
table	*una mesa*

Colours

black	*negro*
blue	*azul*
brown	*marron*
green	*verde*
orange	*naranja*
red	*rojo*
white	*blanco*
yellow	*amarillo*

Numbers

0	*cero*	30	*treinta*
1	*un/una/uno*	40	*cuarenta*
2	*dos*	50	*cincuenta*
3	*tres*	60	*sesenta*
4	*cuatro*	70	*setenta*
5	*cinco*	80	*ochenta*
6	*seis*	90	*noventa*
7	*siete*	100	*cien*
8	*ocho*	101	*ciento uno*
9	*nueve*	110	*ciento diez*
10	*diez*	200	*doscientos*
11	*once*	300	*trescientos*
12	*doce*	400	*quatrocientos*
13	*trece*	500	*quinientos*
14	*catorce*	600	*seiscientos*
15	*quince*	700	*setecientos*
16	*dieciseis*	800	*ochocientos*
17	*diecisiete*	900	*novecientos*
18	*dieciocho*	1.000	*mil*
19	*diecinueve*	2.000	*dos mil*
20	*viente*	3.000	*tres mil*
21	*vientiuno*	1.000.000	*una million*
22	*vientidos*		
23	*vientitres*		
24	*vienticuatro*		
25	*vienticinco*		
26	*vientiseis*		
27	*vientisiete*		
28	*vientiocho*		
29	*vientinueve*		

Days

Monday	*lunes*
Tuesday	*martes*
Wednesday	*miercoles*
Thursday	*jueves*
Friday	*viernes*
Saturday	*sabado*
Sunday	*domingo*
today	*hoy*

Months

January	*enero*	July	*julio*
February	*febrero*	August	*agosto*
March	*marzo*	September	*septiembre*
April	*abril*	October	*octubre*
May	*mayo*	November	*noviembre*
June	*junio*	December	*diciembre*

Seasons

spring	*la primavera*	summer	*el verano*
autumn	*el otono*	winter	*el invierno*

Appendix 11

USEFUL WEB ADDRESSES

International Property Sales

Atlas International	www.atlasinternational.com
David Headland Associates	www.headlands.co.uk
Masa International UK Ltd	www.masainter.com
Propertunities Ltd	www.propertunities.co.uk
Taylor Woodrow	www.taywoodspain.co.uk
Hot Property Costa Blanca	www.hotpropertycostablanca.com

Interpreting

Susana Bultitude	www.susanbultitude.com

Financial planning

Blevins and Franks	www.blevinsfranks.com
Henry Woods	www.henrywoods.com

Sovereign Group	www.sovereigngroup.com

Travel and flights

Air Lingus	www.aerlingus.com
British Airways	www.britishairways.com
Brittany Ferries (Plymouth/Santander)	www.brittanyferries.com
Easy Jet	www.easyJet.com
Eurostar	www.eurostar.com
Eurotunnel	www.eurotunnel.com
GB Airways	www.gbairways.com
Iberia	www.iberia.com
P & O (Portsmouth to Bilbao)	www.poportsmouth.com
Spanish Railways	www.renfe.com
Thomas Cook	www.thomascook.co.uk
Ebookers	www.ebookers.com

Pets

Department of Environment (export of dogs and cats)	www.defra.gov.uk/animalh/quarantine

Retirement

Occupational Pensions Registry www.opra.gov.uk

Pre Retirement Association www.pra.uk.com

UK state pensions www.dss.gov.uk

Taxation

Inland Revenue (former UK tax
payers now living abroad)
Fitzroy House, PO Box 46,
Nottingham NG2 IBD. www.inlandrevenue.gov.uk

Miscellaneous

BBC World Service www.bbc.co.uk/worldservice

British Council www.britishcouncil.es

Stanford's (maps, guides and
travel books) www.stanfords.co.uk

Foreign Office Travel Advice www.fco.gov.uk/travel

Tourist information www.tourspain.es

Information site www.thinkspain.com

Appendix 12

FURTHER READING

Spanish history

Don Quixote: Miguel Cervantes (Penguin). A classic.

Modern Spain: Raymond Carr (Opus). Says it all.

The New Spaniards: John Hooper (Penguin). An excellent work.

The Spanish Civil War: Antony Beevor (Castell). The civil war in perspective.

Spanish culture

Costa del Crime: Wensley Clarkson (Blake). The new alternative culture.

Culture Shock: Marie Louise Graff (Kuperard). A guide to Spanish customs and etiquettes.

Death in the Afternoon: Ernest Hemingway (Grafton). His famous look at bullfighting.

Spanish Vignettes: Norman Berdichevsky (Santana). Cultural topic of interest.

Going to Spain

Best Places to Buy a Home in Spain: Joanna Styles (Survival). All the facts.

Foreigners in Spain: Graeme Chesters (Survival). Triumphs and disasters.

Going to Spain: Harry King (How To Books). Another straightforward guide.

Retire Abroad: Roger Jones (How To Books). Happy retirement abroad.

Learning the language

AA Essential Spanish Phrase Book (AA). Common sense phrases.

Oxford Spanish Starter Dictionary (Oxford University Press).

Suenos World Spanish (BBC). Multi media course for beginners' Spanish.

Viva Espana (BBC). Beginners' language course.

Travel

Eyewitness Spain (Dorling and Kindersley). The best travel guide.

Spain: Facaros and Pauls (Cadogan Guides). A different style.

Special Places to Stay: Alastair Sawday (ASP). A roof off the beaten track.

Sunflower Landscapes (Sunflower Books). Four walking guides for Spain.

Food and wine

Cooking in Spain: Janet Mendal (Santana). The essential cooking book for Spain.

Tapas and more great dishes from Spain: Janet Mendal (Santana). Spain's bar food.

The New Spain: John Radford (Mitchell Beazley). A well-illustrated wine guide.

World Food Spain (Lonely Planet). Buying fun food.

Humour

An Englishman Abroad: Phil Ball (Embury Press). Beckham is everywhere.

Driving Over Lemons: Chris Stewart (Sort of Book). A humorous optimist in Andalusia.

Nord Riley's Spain (Santana). The life of a humorous wanderer.

Spanish Lessons: Derek Lambert (Embury). Beginning a new life in Spain.

Index